GREAT SNACKS
& APPETIZERS

ORLA BRODERICK

PHOTOGRAPHS BY
ROBIN MATTHEWS

RIZZOLI
NEW YORK

CONTENTS

6

Introduction

8

A Well-Stocked Kitchen

12

The Recipes

Hot & Spicy, Fancy Finger Food, Quick & Easy,
Light & Healthy, Bread Bites

62

Recipe Index

INTRODUCTION

There are few things more enjoyable than indulging in snack-attacks. We all have them, sometimes because we're in a hurry, or just because we need something to munch. How often have you had friends visit on the spur of the moment and wanted to offer them something to eat that doesn't take hours to prepare? Or wanted to impress guests with a tantalizing array of canapés? This book offers ideas to suit all occasions.

Divided into five chapters, the recipes are full of interesting tastes and textures, inspired by the wealth of ingredients from all corners of the world. And all of the recipes are easy to make at home. Most are for finger foods, perfect for entertaining without the need for knives and forks or lots of plates.

Now you can entertain friends in style, with a choice of exciting combinations and flavors. Use your imagination and put together a selection of the recipes under a common theme, choosing dishes from the different chapters to make up a Chinese, Indian, or Greek evening, for example. The possibilities are endless!

The equipment required to prepare the recipes is very straightforward, and will be found in most domestic kitchens. The list of essentials includes a good food processor, a sharp cook's knife, a heavy-based skillet, a grater, a citrus squeezer, a measuring cup, a strainer, scissors, a pastry brush, a rolling pin, different sized mixing bowls, a handful of wooden spoons and spatulas, and a selection of metal cutters.

Relying on a snack to take the place of a meal is often necessary, and can be healthy and enjoyable with very little preparation. And, of course, impulse snacking is always a pleasure! This is a book for all of us who love good food and entertaining but have busy, hectic lifestyles.

A WELL-STOCKED KITCHEN

Many of the ingredients used in this book can be found in a well-stocked pantry or cupboard. The list below may seem long, but if you're an enthusiastic cook you'll be amazed at how much you already have. When you're shopping, just add a couple of "extras" to your basket to keep in the cupboard for a rainy day. Most of these items have quite a long shelf life. Do bear in mind, though, that expiration dates need to be observed, and that some foods, once opened, must be refrigerated.

A well-stocked kitchen doesn't mean cramped, poorly organized, *over*-stocked cupboards, in which you don't know what you have or where it is. So be sensible and make the most of the space available to you. For example, a sturdy rack on the wall near the stove can provide room for oils, vinegars, and the sauces and flavorings you use regularly. When deciding where to keep ingredients, choose a spot that is well ventilated and out of direct sunlight. And ensure there is a regular turnover of basic ingredients. Remember that this list is only a guide, and it should be tailored to suit your requirements. Many of the ingredients here, used throughout the book, may not be available at your regular supermarket. Because of the international selection of recipes, some foreign ingredients will only be sold in Chinese, Indian, or other Asian grocery stores. You will be able to buy other ingredients in delicatessens and gourmet food stores.

EXTRA-VIRGIN OLIVE OIL

SUNFLOWER OIL

VEGETABLE OIL

WHITE- AND RED-WINE VINEGARS

BALSAMIC VINEGAR

ENGLISH MUSTARD POWDER

DIJON, WHOLEGRAIN, AND YELLOW MUSTARDS

WORCESTERSHIRE SAUCE

HOT-PEPPER SAUCE

SWEET CHILI SAUCE

GREEN AND RED PESTO SAUCES (BOTTLED)

LIGHT AND DARK SOY SAUCES

TOMATO KETCHUP

SMOOTH AND CRUNCHY PEANUT BUTTER

CREAMED HORSERADISH

TAPENADE (BOTTLED)

RIPE AND GREEN OLIVES

MANGO CHUTNEY

CAYENNE PEPPER AND PAPRIKA

GROUND CUMIN, CORIANDER, AND CHILI POWDER

SMALL DRIED CHILIES

MUSTARD SEED

SAFFRON STRANDS

MILD, MEDIUM, AND HOT CURRY POWDERS

MILD, MEDIUM, AND HOT CURRY PASTES

THAI RED AND GREEN CURRY PASTES

HONEY

CRUSHED TOMATOES (CANNED)

CONCENTRATED TOMATO PASTE

SUN-DRIED TOMATO PASTE (SEE PAGE 40)

SUN-DRIED TOMATOES IN OIL

LIGHT AND DARK BROWN SUGARS

GRANULATED AND SUPERFINE SUGARS

ALL-PURPOSE FLOUR

BAKING POWDER

BAKING SODA

CORNSTARCH

DRIED BREAD CRUMBS

DRIED APRICOTS

DATES

CHINESE NOODLES

SESAME SEEDS

TORTILLA CHIPS

ITALIAN POLENTA OR YELLOW CORNMEAL

BULGUR WHEAT

PICKLED HERRING (BOTTLED)

ARTICHOKE HEARTS (BOTTLED)

MUSTARD RELISH

RED CURRANT JELLY

CHICKPEAS (CANNED)

SWEET RED PEPPERS (PIMIENTOS)

ANCHOVY FILLETS IN OIL (CANNED)

TUNA IN WATER OR OIL (CANNED)

COCONUT MILK (CANNED)

BLOCK OF CREAMED COCONUT

GRAPE LEAVES IN BRINE

THE BASICS

IN THE REFRIGERATOR

The cook's life is made much easier if the following essentials are always on hand in the refrigerator. Most of these foods will keep well if stored in the correct conditions. For example, wrap cheese individually in plastic wrap or foil, and use fresh wrapping for further storage after each use. Because eggs absorb odors very easily, keep them away from any strong-smelling foods in the refrigerator, and store them pointed end downward in their box or in the door of the refrigerator.

Try to buy unwaxed or organic citrus fruits, particularly if you are going to use the peel, and keep them in the salad compartment at the bottom of the refrigerator, along with the vegetables. (If you only find waxed citrus fruits, scrub the skin in warm soapy water and rinse well before use.) Chilies, scallions, and fresh gingerroot keep best in airtight plastic bags in the refrigerator. It's also a good idea to wash and dry them before storage.

UNSALTED BUTTER	*PARMESAN CHEESE*	*FRESH RED AND GREEN CHILIES*
MILK	*CHEDDAR AND GRUYERE CHEESES*	*ONIONS, SCALLIONS, AND SHALLOTS*
EGGS	*GOAT CHEESE*	
CREME FRAICHE AND FROMAGE FRAIS	*MAYONNAISE*	*FRESH GINGERROOT*
PLAIN YOGURT, INCLUDING THE THICK VARIETY	*BACON*	*CUCUMBERS*
	LEMONS AND LIMES	*TOMATOES*

IN THE FREEZER

Pack away this small list of basics in the freezer and you'll find yourself ready for all manner of emergencies. In addition, you can have a couple of prepared dishes on standby—throughout the book, all the recipes that freeze well are indicated. Another good tip is to freeze a proportion of the appetizers you make each time you entertain. That way you can present your next guests with a much wider selection without extra effort!

PIECRUST PASTRY DOUGH	*WHOLE-KERNEL CORN*	*WHITE CRAB MEAT*
PUFF PASTRY DOUGH	*PEAS*	*PITA BREAD*
PHYLLO PASTRY DOUGH	*SLICED SMOKED SALMON OR TROUT*	*ENGLISH MUFFINS*
WHITE BREAD CRUMBS	*KIPPERS OR OTHER SMOKED FISH*	*WHOLE-WHEAT AND/OR WHITE BREAD*
LEAF SPINACH	*LARGE AND JUMBO SHRIMP*	

ON THE WINDOWSILL

Whenever possible, use fresh herbs for their powerful and pungent flavors. Buying them in small plastic packages from the supermarket or greengrocer can be very expensive, so try growing a good selection of herbs on the windowsill. They also brighten up the kitchen.

Parsley and chives are essential, while basil, thyme, mint, tarragon, rosemary, dill, and oregano are also useful. Herbs just need to be watered occasionally to thrive, and picking the new shoots encourages the rest of the plant to fill out.

IN THE VEGETABLE BIN

Vegetables with a very long shelf life include potatoes, shallots, onions, carrots, and garlic. No doubt you already have a high turnover of most of these. For storage, remove them from their original packaging and discard any damaged produce to prevent further decay. All these vegetables will keep well in a cool, dark place, such as a garage or shed, preferably stored on individual wire racks. Onions, shallots, and garlic can also be hung up in bunches in any dry, airy place. Braids of these vegetables make an attractive kitchen ornament, but exposure to the light and humidity of a kitchen will diminish their keeping power and flavor. Covered terracotta containers with ventilation holes offer an alternative storage method that is both attractive and practical where cupboard space is limited.

Always buy the freshest vegetables you can find and make the most of seasonal produce. Not only does it taste great, but it will also be very reasonable in price. Nowadays it's difficult to know what is in season, because most fresh ingredients seem to be available all year round, so don't be afraid to get to know your grocer and ask his or her advice—you'll be an expert in no time at all!

IN THE BAR CABINET

A well-stocked bar cabinet may seem an extravagance, but it is a real asset to any cook. Having a selection available will encourage you to experiment with different flavorings—just a dash of something can make all the difference to a dish.

It is always a good idea to have a bottle of red or dry white cooking wine on hand, but skimping on the quality will lessen the flavor of the final dish. Half bottles are ideal for this purpose, and they can be sealed for storage with an airtight vacuum seal, especially designed to prolong the shelf life of opened wines.

Unlike wine, it's perfectly acceptable to use cheaper, unknown brands of spirits in cooking. Some liquor stores cater to this with generic brands of the basics like brandy, rum, vermouth, and sherry, sold at reasonable prices. Miniatures are also very handy to have on hand, particularly of the spirits and liqueurs you don't use too often. But remember that alcohol, like many other ingredients, has an expiration date, and beyond that time it won't add much flavor to your cooking.

THE RECIPES

HOT & SPICY

These recipes are drawn from all around the globe, and are perfect for anyone who likes food with a bit of a kick. Since hotness is very much a matter of personal taste, always use chilies with caution. They vary enormously in strength, but appearance can provide some clues. Dark green chilies are usually hotter than pale green or red ones, and the sharply pointed thin chilies tend to be hotter than short blunt ones. The latter were used in testing the recipes. All recipes serve 4–6.

THAI CRAB BITES WITH SPICED COCONUT DIP

To make this in advance, arrange the cooked crab bites on a baking tray and the dip in a bowl, then leave to cool completely. Cover with plastic wrap and chill for up to 24 hours (the crab bites can also be frozen). Reheat the crab bites at 400°F for about 10 minutes.

1 pound white crabmeat, thawed and well drained if frozen
1 stalk lemongrass, finely chopped
2 red chilies, seeded and chopped
2 tablespoons chopped fresh cilantro
1 egg yolk
2 tablespoons heavy cream
1 teaspoon cornstarch
vegetable oil, for deep-frying

FOR THE SPICED COCONUT DIP
1 tablespoon sesame oil
4 finely chopped scallions
1 tablespoon Thai red curry paste
1 can (14 oz.) coconut milk
1 tablespoon light soy sauce

Place the crabmeat in a bowl with the lemongrass, chilies, cilantro and egg yolk. Heat the cream with the cornstarch over medium heat until thickened, and stir into the crab mixture until well combined. Shape into about 20 walnut-size balls, squeezing out any excess moisture. Place on a plate and chill for at least 15 minutes, or up to 12 hours, to let the balls firm up.

Meanwhile, make the spiced coconut dip. Heat the oil in a saucepan and sauté the scallions for 30 seconds. Stir in the curry paste and cook for 1 minute. Pour in the coconut milk and bring to a boil. Simmer for 15 to 20 minutes, or until reduced by half and thickened. Stir in the soy sauce, pour into a serving bowl, and leave to cool.

Heat oil to 350°F, or until a cube of bread will brown in 30 seconds. Deep-fry the crab bites in batches for 3 to 4 minutes, or until crisp and golden brown. Remove with a slotted spoon and drain on paper towels. Serve warm, with the dip.

POLENTA CRACKERS WITH ROASTED TOMATO SALSA

These crackers are based on an old-fashioned recipe. They are the perfect foil for the richness of the roasted tomato salsa. Roasting tomatoes intensifies and almost caramelizes their flavor—you'll be hooked once you've tried them!

1 1/2 cups yellow cornmeal or polenta
1/2 teaspoon chili powder
4 tablespoons butter, melted, plus extra for greasing

FOR THE ROASTED TOMATO SALSA
1 pound ripe plum tomatoes
2 shallots, peeled
2 garlic cloves, peeled
1 red chili, halved and seeded
salt and freshly ground black pepper
3 tablespoons extra-virgin olive oil
1/2 teaspoon chopped fresh rosemary needles
Juice of 1 lemon
1 teaspoon sugar

Preheat the oven to 400°F. To make the salsa, place the tomatoes, shallots, garlic, and chili in a roasting pan. Season well and roast for 40 to 45 minutes, or until the tomatoes have started to blacken.

Meanwhile, put 3 cups water in a saucepan with a good pinch of salt and bring to a boil. Pour in the cornmeal or polenta in a continuous stream, stirring constantly to prevent any lumps from forming. Add the chili powder. Cook for 5 minutes, stirring constantly, then remove from the heat.

Stir in the butter. Spoon heaped tablespoons of the cornmeal mixture on to large buttered baking trays—you should make about 20 crackers. Bake for 25 to 30 minutes, or until the edges are crisp and beginning to brown. Transfer to wire racks and leave to cool and crisp.

When the tomatoes are ready, scoop out all the seeds and juice. Chop the pulp with the shallots, garlic, and chili, discarding any burned bits. Place in a small serving bowl and add the oil, rosemary, lemon juice, sugar, and any juices from the pan. Season generously. Serve at room temperature with the crackers.

Sweet Potato Slices with Chili–Butter Dip

VEGETABLE TEMPURA WITH CHILI DIPPING SAUCE

The beer in this batter makes a wonderful light, crisp coating for the vegetables. You can, however, substitute chilled water.

2 eggs
1¹/4 cups chilled beer
1¹/2 cups all-purpose flour, plus
extra for coating the vegetables
4 small zucchini
2 large red bell peppers, halved and seeded
1 pound broccoli
Vegetable oil, for deep-frying

FOR THE CHILI DIPPING SAUCE
6 tablespoons light soy sauce
1 fresh red chili, seeded and minced
1 teaspoon sugar
1-inch piece fresh gingerroot, finely shredded

To make the sauce, mix together the soy sauce, chili, sugar, and ginger and pour into a small serving bowl. To make the batter, lightly whisk together the eggs and beer. Tip in the measured flour all at once and whisk quickly until the batter is smooth.

Cut the zucchini in half crosswise, then cut each half into 4 sticks. Cut each pepper half into 12 strips. Break the broccoli into florets.

Heat the oil to 350°F or until a cube of bread will brown in 30 seconds. While the oil is heating, place a little flour on a plate.

Coat the vegetables lightly with flour, then dip them into the batter. Deep-fry in batches for 3 to 4 minutes until crisp and golden. Drain on paper towels. Serve at once, with the dipping sauce.

MEXICAN LAMB FAJITAS

Different vegetable combinations, such as baby corn, scallions, or carrot or celery sticks, also work well in this recipe. To make sun-dried tomato paste, see Sizzling Chorizo and Cherry Kabobs, page 40.

1 pound lean lamb tenderloin or leg
2 garlic cloves, crushed
2 teaspoons chili powder
2 teaspoons sun-dried tomato paste
2 tablespoons sunflower oil
1 large onion, thickly sliced

1 red and 1 yellow bell pepper, seeded and sliced
1 zucchini, cut into matchsticks
Salt and freshly ground black pepper
8 soft flour tortillas
¹/2 cup sour cream

Cut the lamb into thin slices, discarding any fat, and place in a bowl. Add the garlic, chili powder, and sun-dried tomato paste and stir.

Heat the oil in a large pan and cook the lamb for 4 to 5 minutes until lightly browned. Add the onion, peppers, and zucchini and stir-fry for 3 to 4 minutes longer until the onion is just cooked tender. Season.

Wrap the flour tortillas in a dish towel and place in a steamer for a couple of minutes to heat through. Spoon some of the lamb mixture down the middle of each tortilla. Drizzle each one with a tablespoon of the sour cream, then roll up and cut in half to serve.

SWEET POTATO SLICES WITH CHILI–BUTTER DIP

There are two varieties of sweet potato—the pale-fleshed ones, often called yams in the U.S., and the bright orange ones. Both are suitable for this recipe, although the orange-fleshed variety are sweeter.

4 sweet potatoes, each about 8 ounces
Vegetable oil, for deep-frying

FOR THE CHILI–BUTTER DIP
6 tablespoons unsalted butter
1 garlic clove, crushed
1 small shallot, finely chopped
2 small fresh red chilies, seeded and minced

1 teaspoon sun-dried tomato paste
2 tablespoons chopped mixed fresh herbs, such as thyme, parsley, and chives
Salt and freshly ground black pepper

Peel the sweet potatoes and cut lengthwise into slices about ¹/4 inch thick. Rinse well and dry with paper towels. Heat the oil to 350°F or until a cube of bread will brown in 30 seconds.

While the oil is heating, make the chili-butter dip. Melt the butter in a small pan. Add the garlic, shallot, chilies, and sun-dried tomato paste and cook over very low heat for about 5 minutes until the shallot is tender. Remove the pan from the heat, stir in the herbs, and season to taste. Pour into a small bowl and leave at room temperature, but don't leave for too long or the butter will become hard.

Add the sweet potato slices to the hot oil and deep fry for 4 to 5 minutes until tender and golden. Remove with a slotted spoon and drain well on paper towels. Arrange on a serving platter and season to taste. Serve hot, with the chili-butter dip.

GUACAMOLE WITH ROASTED PEPPERS AND CHILI TORTILLA CHIPS

If you want to make the guacamole in advance, drizzle a little extra lime juice over the surface and cover tightly with plastic wrap.

1 small red and 1 small yellow bell pepper	1/2 teaspoon each garlic salt and chili powder
1 large ripe avocado	1 package (8-ounce) chili-flavored tortilla chips
1 cup seeded and diced tomatoes	
2 scallions, minced	
Juice of 1 lime	

Preheat the broiler. Cut the peppers in half and then into quarters. Remove the seeds. Broil, skin side up, until the skins are charred. Remove from the heat and leave to cool a little, then pull away the skins and cut the flesh into small dice.

Cut the avocado in half and remove the pit. Scoop the flesh into a nonmetallic dish and mash to a fairly smooth purée. Stir in the diced peppers, tomatoes, and scallions. Add the lime juice, garlic salt, and chili powder and stir together. Cover and chill until ready to serve, with the tortilla chips.

VEGETABLE BHAJIAS WITH TOMATO CHUTNEY

These can be made and cooked several hours in advance. Just before serving, reheat the bhajias in a preheated 400°F oven for 8 to 10 minutes. Or, you can deep-fry them for 1 to 2 minutes.

1 cup gram flour (chickpea flour), plus extra for dusting	FOR THE TOMATO CHUTNEY
1/2 teaspoon baking soda	2 tablespoons vegetable oil
2 teaspoons medium-hot curry powder	2 teaspoons cumin seeds
Vegetable oil, for deep-frying	1 large onion, chopped
1 eggplant, sliced crosswise	1 can (14-ounce) crushed tomatoes
1 sweet potato, peeled and sliced crosswise	2 tablespoons sugar
1 pound cauliflower, broken into small florets	1 tablespoon red-wine vinegar
	Salt and freshly ground black pepper

Sift the flour, baking soda, curry powder, and a pinch of salt into a large bowl. Gradually stir in 1 cup water to make a smooth batter. Cover and leave to rest for 15 minutes.

Meanwhile, make the chutney. Heat the oil in a saucepan and cook the cumin seeds for 20 seconds or until they start to splutter. Add the onion and sauté gently until soft. Stir in the tomatoes, sugar, and vinegar and season generously. Simmer for 15 minutes or until reduced and thicker. Remove the pan from the heat and leave to cool.

Heat the oil to 350°F or until a cube of bread will brown in 30 seconds. While the oil is heating, cut the eggplant and sweet potato slices in half to make half-moons. Place a little gram flour on a plate.

Dust all the vegetables in gram flour, then dip them in the batter. Deep-fry in batches for 5 minutes or until golden. Remove with a slotted spoon and drain on paper towels. Serve hot, with the chutney.

CHINESE EGG ROLLS

Wonton skins, used to make egg rolls, are sold fresh or frozen in supermarkets and Oriental food stores. They come in a variety of sizes and 8-inch squares are best for this recipe.

1 tablespoon sunflower oil	1 tablespoon soy sauce,
1 garlic clove, minced	1/2 teaspoon sugar
1/2-inch piece fresh gingerroot, minced	5 ounces bean sprouts
6 scallions, minced	12 wonton skins, thawed if frozen
8 ounces cooked shelled shrimp	Vegetable oil, for deep-frying

Heat the oil in a small pan and sauté the garlic and ginger for 1 minute. Add the scallions, shrimp, soy sauce, and sugar and cook for 1 to 2 minutes, stirring continuously. Add the bean sprouts and stir-fry for 30 seconds longer. Remove the pan from the heat, tip the contents into a strainer and leave to drain—the mixture must be very dry.

Place one of the wonton skins on the counter at an angle with one corner pointing toward you. Spoon a heaped tablespoon of the filling near the bottom corner. Fold up the bottom and fold in the sides, then roll upward from the bottom. Moisten the flap with a little water and press to seal. Repeat to fill and shape the remaining egg rolls.

Heat the oil to 350°F or until a cube of bread will brown in 30 seconds. Deep-fry for 2 to 3 minutes until crisp and golden brown all over. Remove with a slotted spoon and drain on paper towels. Serve hot, with extra soy sauce for dipping.

Vegetable Tempura with Chili Dipping Sauce

17

POTATO WEDGES WITH FRESH CILANTRO CHUTNEY

You can make this chutney even quicker using a food processor—just put all the ingredients in the bowl without chopping first and blend until a thick paste forms.

2 tablespoons sunflower oil
4 baking potatoes, about 8 ounces each
2 teaspoons hot curry powder
1 teaspoon kosher salt

FOR THE CHUTNEY
1/2 cup chopped fresh cilantro
1 shallot, finely chopped
Juice of 1 lemon
1/2 teaspoon chili powder
1 teaspoon ground cumin

Preheat the oven to 400°F. Heat the oil in a roasting pan in the oven for 5 minutes. Meanwhile, cut each potato into 8 wedges, rinse under cold running water, and pat dry with paper towels.

Add the potato wedges to the roasting pan. Toss until well coated in oil and sprinkle with curry powder. Roast for 30 to 35 minutes until golden brown, turning the wedges over after 15 minutes.

Meanwhile, make the chutney. Mix together the cilantro, shallot, lemon juice, chili powder, and cumin in a small serving bowl.

When the potatoes are cooked through and tender, sprinkle with the salt and serve hot, with the chutney.

SPICED LAMB KABOBS WITH TZATZIKI

Using a food processor can save a lot of time in preparing this recipe. Simply process the lamb, onion, and parsley together, then add the remaining ingredients and process again to make a sticky paste.

1 pound lean ground lamb
1 onion, minced
1/2 cup chopped fresh parsley
1 teaspoon ground coriander
1/2 teaspoon each apple pie spice and chili powder

FOR THE TZATZIKI
2/3 cup plain yogurt
4-inch piece cucumber, seeded and diced
2 tablespoons chopped fresh mint
1 garlic clove, crushed
Salt and freshly ground black pepper

To make the tzatziki, place the yogurt, cucumber, mint, and garlic in a small bowl and stir together. Season to taste. Cover with plastic wrap and chill until ready to use.

Put the lamb, onion, and parsley in a bowl and mix until well combined. Add the coriander, apple pie spice, and chili powder. Season generously and mix well again.

Preheat the broiler. Divide the lamb mixture into 8 portions and roll each into a sausage shape about 4 inches long. Thread each one onto a metal skewer at least 6 inches long. Broil for 8 to 10 minutes, turning each kabob occasionally, until cooked through but still moist. Serve hot, with the tzatziki for dipping.

HOT-AND-SOUR NOODLE-WRAPPED SHRIMP

Large raw shrimp are sold at the fish counter in supermarkets and from specialist fish merchants. However, if you can't find raw shrimp, use large cooked shelled shrimp and broil for just 2 to 3 minutes.

1 pound raw large or jumbo shrimp
2 fresh red chilies, seeded and minced
2 garlic cloves, crushed
1 stalk lemongrass, crushed
2 tablespoons chopped fresh cilantro

Juice of 3 limes
2 tablespoons light soy sauce
2 teaspoons sesame oil
1 ounce dried medium egg noodles

Shell the shrimp, leaving the shells on the tails. Mix together the chilies, garlic, lemongrass, cilantro, lime juice, soy sauce, and sesame oil in a shallow nonmetallic bowl. Add the shrimp and stir until they are coated all over. Cover and chill for at least 15 minutes or up to 1 hour.

Cook the noodles in a pan of boiling salted water for 1 minute or until just tender. Drain and refresh in cold water. Wrap a piece of noodle around each shrimp and arrange on a lightly greased baking sheet.

Place the remaining marinade in a small pan and bring to a boil. Lower the heat and simmer for 1 to 2 minutes. Pour into a serving bowl and leave to cool.

Preheat the broiler. Broil the shrimp for 5 to 6 minutes, turning each one over once, until they just cook through and turn pink. Serve at once, with the dipping sauce.

CHINESE-SPICED SPARERIBS

In this recipe the ribs are simmered to tenderize the meat before being roasted in a spicy sauce. Give each guest a finger bowl of warm water and plenty of napkins because eating ribs is a messy business.

2 pounds meaty pork spareribs
2 tablespoons red-wine vinegar
1 tablespoon sesame oil
2 garlic cloves, crushed
1-inch piece fresh gingerroot, crushed

1 teaspoon Chinese five-spice powder
6 tablespoons dark soy sauce
Juice of 1 lemon
4 tablespoons honey

Place the ribs in a large saucepan and pour in enough water to cover. Add the vinegar and bring to a boil. Lower the heat and simmer for 20 minutes, skimming the surface occasionally to remove any foam. Drain well and transfer the ribs to a large roasting pan.

Preheat the oven to 400°F. Heat the oil in a small pan and stir-fry the garlic and ginger for 10 seconds. Add the Chinese five-spice powder and stir-fry for 10 seconds longer. Add the soy sauce, lemon juice, honey, and 1/2 cup water. Bring to a boil, then simmer for 5 minutes or until reduced and slightly thicker.

Pour the sauce over the ribs and turn them over so they are evenly coated. Roast for about 1 hour, basting every 10 minutes. Leave to cool for 5 minutes before serving.

CORN AND CHILI CORNBREAD MUFFINS

To use fresh corn in this recipe, hold the thick end of the cob upright with the tapered end on a chopping board. Use a sharp knife to slice off the kernels. You can also use well-drained canned corn kernels.

1¹/₄ cups all-purpose flour	1¹/₄ cups buttermilk
1 tablespoon baking powder	2 tablespoons sunflower oil, plus extra
1 teaspoon salt	1 heaping cup corn kernels, thawed if frozen
²/₃ cup yellow cornmeal	2 green chilies, seeded and minced
2 eggs, beaten	¹/₂ cup freshly grated Parmesan cheese

Preheat the oven to 400°F. Sift the flour, baking powder, and salt into a large bowl. Stir in the cornmeal. Mix together the eggs, buttermilk, and oil, then stir into the dry ingredients. Add the corn, chilies, and Parmesan cheese and stir until well combined.

Put paper muffin cases into 20 holes on muffin trays and brush each with extra oil. Spoon in the batter, almost filling each paper case. Bake 25 to 30 minutes until risen and golden. Serve warm or at room temperature.

FRIED CAULIFLOWER FLORETS WITH ROMESCO SAUCE

This traditional Spanish sauce has many variations. Its sharp flavor complements the crisp, marinated cauliflower.

4¹/₂ cups cauliflower florets	¹/₂ cup olive oil
4 tablespoons white-wine vinegar	2 garlic cloves, crushed
4 tablespoons chopped fresh parsley	1 fresh red chili, seeded and minced
Salt and freshly ground black pepper	1 slice stale white bread, broken into pieces
1 red bell pepper, seeded and quartered	¹/₂ cup slivered almonds, toasted
8 ounces small tomatoes	2 eggs, beaten

Put the cauliflower florets in a large bowl. Sprinkle with half the vinegar, half the parsley, and 2 tablespoons water. Season to taste and stir well. Cover with plastic wrap and set aside for at least 15 minutes, and up to 30 minutes, stirring occasionally.

Meanwhile, make the romesco sauce. Preheat the broiler. Broil the pepper and tomatoes until the skins are charred. Let cool slightly, then remove the skins. Halve, core, and seed the pepper. Cut the tomatoes in half and scoop out the seeds. Chop the pepper and tomatoes.

Heat 2 tablespoons of the oil in a skillet and sauté the garlic and chili for 1 to 2 minutes. Add the bread and sauté until lightly browned. Place the bread mixture in a food processor with the tomatoes, pepper, the remaining vinegar, the remaining parsley, and the almonds. Blend to a rough purée. Then, with the motor running, add 4 tablespoons of the oil in a steady stream. Pour the sauce into a small serving bowl and season to taste.

Heat the remaining oil in a large skillet. Drain the cauliflower, pat dry, and dip into the beaten eggs. Stir-fry for about 10 minutes until tender and light golden. Serve at once, with the romesco sauce.

EMPANADAS

These can be made up to 24 hours in advance, left to cool, covered with plastic wrap, and chilled until required. Don't worry if they become a little soggy—they will crisp up again when they are reheated. To serve, reheat in a 400°F oven for 8 to 10 minutes.

1 tablespoon sunflower oil	FOR THE PASTRY DOUGH
1 fresh red and 1 green chili, seeded and minced	1¹/₂ cups all-purpose flour
1 teaspoon cumin seeds	1 teaspoon salt
1¹/₂ cups corn kernels, thawed if frozen	¹/₄ cup shortening, diced
2 plum tomatoes, peeled, seeded, and diced	
¹/₂ cup grated Cheddar cheese	
Salt and freshly ground black pepper	
Vegetable oil, for frying	

To make the pastry dough, sift the flour and salt into a bowl and cut in the fat. Gradually add ²/₃ cup warm water and mix to make a soft dough. Turn out onto a lightly floured counter and knead for 2 to 3 minutes. Wrap in plastic wrap and chill for 15 minutes.

Meanwhile, heat the sunflower oil in a pan and sauté the chilies and cumin for 2 minutes. Remove from the heat and stir in the corn, tomatoes, and cheese. Leave to cool. Season to taste.

Roll out the dough on a lightly floured board and stamp out 20 circles, using a 4-inch round cutter. Place a tablespoon of the corn mixture on each circle. Dampen the edges with water, then fold in half and press the edges together to seal.

Heat about ¹/₂ inch oil in a skillet and fry the empanadas in batches for about 5 minutes, turning them over once, until golden brown. Remove with a slotted spoon and drain on paper towels. Serve hot.

DEVILED CHICKEN WINGS

Chicken wings are inexpensive and make great finger food—just make sure you have plenty of napkins for sticky fingers!

3 tablespoons tomato ketchup	1 teaspoon light brown sugar
1 tablespoon bottled chili sauce	1 teaspoon prepared English mustard
1 teaspoon Worcestershire sauce	12 chicken wings
2 garlic cloves, crushed	

Put the tomato ketchup, chili sauce, Worcestershire sauce, garlic, sugar, and mustard in a shallow nonmetallic dish and stir together.

Remove the thin, pointed tip from each chicken wing, leaving just the elbow and mini drumstick. Add the chicken wings to the marinade and turn each one over to coat on both sides. Cover with plastic wrap and chill for at least 15 minutes or up to 24 hours.

Preheat the broiler. Shake off any excess marinade from the chicken wings and place them on the broiler rack over the broiler pan. Broil for 15 to 20 minutes, turning them over occasionally, until cooked through. Serve hot.

MINI SAMOSAS WITH MINT AND CILANTRO CHUTNEY

Phyllo pastry dough is so thin it is almost transparent, and it can be difficult to handle. Keep the sheets you aren't working with covered with a damp dish towel, to prevent them from cracking or drying out.

6 tablespoons sunflower oil
1 garlic clove, crushed
1/2-inch piece fresh gingerroot, crushed
2 1/2 cups diced peeled potatoes
1 tablespoon medium curry paste
1/2 cup peas, thawed if frozen
4 sheets phyllo pastry dough, thawed if frozen

FOR THE CHUTNEY
1/4 cup each chopped fresh mint and cilantro
1 fresh red chili, seeded and minced
Juice of 1 lime
1 teaspoon garam masala or curry powder

Preheat the oven to 400°F. Heat half the oil in a skillet and cook the garlic and ginger for 10 seconds. Add the potatoes, stir well, cover, and cook for 10 minutes or until tender, stirring frequently.

Stir in the curry paste and peas and cook for 2 to 3 minutes longer. Remove the pan from the heat and leave to cool completely.

Meanwhile, make the chutney. Mix together the mint, cilantro, chili, lime juice, and garam masala or curry powder in a bowl. Set aside.

Cut each sheet of phyllo pastry dough into 3 equal pieces. Working with one piece at a time, place a tablespoon of the vegetable mixture at one end. Brush the edges lightly with oil. Fold a bottom corner diagonally over the filling, then fold this triangle over on itself 2 times to make a neat package. Repeat to make 12 samosas.

Place the samosas on a lightly greased baking sheet and brush with the remaining oil. Bake for about 20 minutes until crisp and golden brown. Serve hot, with the chutney.

TURKEY WONTONS

These are a Chinese-style version of ravioli. You will find wonton skins in the Oriental section of large supermarkets and Chinese food stores. Look for ones that are 3 inches square for this recipe.

1 tablespoons sunflower oil
4 scallions, minced
1/2 cup finely chopped cooked turkey breast
1/2 cup chopped mung bean sprouts
2 garlic cloves, crushed
1-inch piece fresh gingerroot, crushed
1 tablespoon light soy sauce, plus extra
1 teaspoon honey
1 teaspoon sesame oil
20 wonton skins, thawed if frozen

Heat the sunflower oil in a pan and stir-fry the scallions for 10 seconds. Transfer to a bowl and stir in the turkey, bean sprouts, garlic, ginger, soy sauce, honey, and sesame oil.

Place a heaped teaspoon of the turkey mixture into the middle of a wonton skin. Dampen the edges with water and bring 2 opposite edges up to the middle. Bring up the remaining edges to form a purse shape, pinching to seal. Repeat to make 20 wontons.

Place the wontons in a layer in a lightly oiled steamer and steam for 6 to 8 minutes until heated through. Serve with soy sauce for dipping.

PLANTAIN FRIES WITH TAMARIND CHUTNEY

Indian and Thai food stores sell tamarind paste in jars, as well as semidried tamarind in blocks. The latter needs to be broken up, soaked in boiling water, and pushed through a strainer to make a thick paste.

2 unripe green plantains, peeled and thinly sliced
Vegetable oil, for deep-frying

FOR THE TAMARIND CHUTNEY
2 tablespoons sunflower oil
1 onion, minced
2 green chilies, seeded and minced
2-inch piece fresh gingerroot, minced
1 teaspoon hot curry paste
5 tablespoons tamarind paste
1 teaspoon salt
1 tablespoon light brown sugar

Rinse the plantains in cold water and pat dry. Heat oil to 350°F or until a bread cube will brown in 30 seconds. Deep-fry the plantain slices in batches for 4 to 5 minutes until cooked and pale golden brown. Drain on paper towels and leave to cool.

To make the chutney, heat the oil in a pan and sauté the onion, chilies, and ginger for 4 to 5 minutes until the onion is tender. Stir in the curry paste and cook for one minute longer. Stir in the tamarind paste, salt, sugar, and 2/3 cup water. Simmer for 10 to15 minutes until thick. Leave to cool, then serve with the plantain fries.

MIXED SATAY SKEWERS

Look for Laos powder in Asian food stores. It is ground greater galangal, a rhizome related to ginger, and imparts a peppery flavor.

1/2 boneless chicken breast, skinned
6 ounces each sirloin and pork tenderloin
1 garlic clove, crushed
1 tablespoon light brown sugar
1 tablespoon Laos powder
4 tablespoons coconut milk
Salt and freshly ground white pepper

FOR THE PEANUT SAUCE
1 1/4 cups coconut milk
4 tablespoons peanut butter
2 tablespoons Thai green curry paste
2 tablespoons light brown sugar
Juice of 1 lime

Using a sharp knife, cut the chicken breast half in half crosswise, then in half lengthwise, to make 4 pieces. Cut the steak and pork into 1-inch slices on the diagonal. Place all the meat between 2 sheets of plastic wrap and beat with a rolling pin to flatten. Cut each piece in half lengthwise and place in a shallow nonmetallic dish.

Mix together the garlic, sugar, Laos powder, coconut milk, and seasoning to make a fairly thick paste. Spoon over the meat and stir each piece to coat. Marinate for at least 15 minutes or up to 24 hours.

To make the sauce, place all the ingredients in a pan and bring to a boil. Lower the heat and simmer for 10 minutes or until thick. Season to taste, remove from the heat, and leave to cool.

Preheat the broiler. Thread the meat onto 6-inch bamboo skewers and brush with a little oil. Broil for about 10 minutes, turning the skewers frequently, until cooked through. Serve hot, with the peanut sauce.

Mini Samosas with Mint and Cilantro Chutney

FANCY FINGER FOOD

Small nibbles can take hours of preparation, only to be devoured by guests in moments. The great thing about the recipes in this chapter is that you can prepare most of them, ready to cook, up to 24 hours in advance, or you can have them tucked away in the freezer, ready for any surprise. As a general rule, when entertaining allow about 12 pieces per person, and prepare a selection of recipes to give variety. Arrange them on large serving platters, mixing the colors, shapes, and flavors. Give your guests cocktail napkins, and leave small plates around so it is easy to discard breadcrusts and toothpicks. Most recipes make 24 pieces.

SALT COD FRITTERS WITH SWEET PEPPER SAUCE

To prepare this several hours in advance, make the dip, cover, and chill until needed. Cook the fritters and drain well on paper towels. Cover, and chill. Just before serving, reheat the fritters in a 400°F oven for about 5 minutes.

1¹/2 pounds salt cod	FOR THE SWEET PEPPER SAUCE
2¹/2 cups milk	2 tabespoons olive oil
¹/2 cup all-purpose flour, plus extra	4 large garlic cloves
¹/2 cup beer	1 can (14-ounce) pimientos, rinsed and
1 egg, beaten	drained
2 tablespoons chopped fresh parsley	4 tablespoons fromage frais
Vegetable oil, for deep-frying	Salt and freshly ground black pepper

Rinse the salt cod under cold running water, then place in a bowl and cover with cold water. Leave to soak for 12 hours, changing the water every couple of hours. Drain, rinse again under cold running water, and pat dry with paper towels. Remove the skin and cut the flesh into 24 cubes. Place in a bowl, pour 2 cups of the milk over, and leave for 2 hours. Drain, rinse again, and pat dry.

To make the sweet pepper sauce, heat the olive oil in a pan and sauté the unpeeled garlic cloves for 2 to 3 minutes until golden. Stir in 2 tablespoons water, cover, and simmer for 15 minutes or until the garlic is completely soft. Squeeze the garlic flesh into a food processor and add the pimientos and fromage frais. Blend until smooth and season to taste. Transfer to a small serving bowl, cover, and chill until required.

Sift the flour and 1 teaspoon salt into a large bowl and make a well in the middle. Gradually beat in the remaining milk, beer, and egg to make a smooth batter. Stir in the parsley. Leave to rest for 30 minutes.

Heat the oil to 350°F or until a cube of bread will brown in 30 seconds. Dust the salt cod cubes in flour, dip into the batter, and deep-fry in batches for about 5 minutes until crisp and golden brown. Drain on paper towels and serve warm, with the sauce.

MINI BOEUF EN CROÛTE

These can be made several hours in advance and popped in the oven to bake just before serving. Once they are out of the oven, however, serve them within a few minutes because the pastry will become soggy if it is left standing for too long.

1 large onion	2 tablespoons brandy
8 ounces open-cap mushrooms	Salt and freshly ground black pepper
2 tablespoons butter	18 ounces puff pastry dough, thawed if
1¹/2 pounds beef tenderloin, in one piece	frozen
1 tablespoon sunflower oil, plus extra	1 egg, beaten
for greasing	

Place the onion and mushrooms in a food processor and blend until very finely chopped. Melt the butter in a pan and slowly fry the onion and mushroom mixture for 10 to 15 minutes until all the liquid evaporates. Remove the pan from the heat and leave to cool.

Trim the beef and cut into 24 cubes, 1¹/2 inches wide and ¹/2 inch thick. Heat the oil in a heavy-based skillet until very hot and cook the beef for about 5 seconds on each side until sealed. It is best to do this in batches. Leave to cool completely, then brush with the brandy and season well.

Roll out the dough on a lightly floured board until ¹/8 inch thick and cut into 4-inch squares. Brush each square lightly with beaten egg and place ¹/2 teaspoon of the onion mixture in the middle. Add a cube of beef and top with ¹/2 teaspoon of the onion mixture.

Pat each mound of filling into a neat shape. Bring 2 opposite corners of dough up to overlap in the middle, tucking in the sides. Brush the dough all over with more beaten egg and bring the remaining 2 corners up to overlap each other. Seal firmly and and chill for at least 30 minutes or up to 24 hours.

Preheat the oven to 425°F with 2 baking sheets inside. When the baking sheets are hot, brush them with oil and sprinkle lightly with water. Arrange the beef packages on the baking sheets and bake for 10 to 15 minutes until golden brown. Serve hot.

Pancetta and Gruyère Tartlets

PANCETTA AND GRUYÈRE TARTLETS

These tartlets can be frozen for up to one month after they have been left to cool. Pancetta is Italian bacon, available from delicatessens and Italian food stores. If you are unable to find any, use rinded slab bacon.

7 ounces phyllo pastry dough, thawed if frozen	1¹/2 cups finely chopped pancetta
4 tablespoons butter, melted	4 eggs, beaten
1¹/2 cups finely grated Gruyère cheese	³/4 cup milk
1 tablespoon olive oil	6 tablespoons heavy cream
2 garlic cloves, crushed	Salt and freshly ground black pepper

Preheat the oven to 350°F. Cut the sheets of phyllo pastry into twenty-four 3-inch squares and keep covered with a damp dish towel. Place each phyllo square in a mold on a muffin tray and brush with a little of the butter. Layer another 2 phyllo squares in each mold, arranging them at angles to make a star effect and brushing each one with butter as you layer it. Sprinkle with half of the Gruyère cheese.

Heat the oil in a small skillet and sauté the garlic for 1 minute. Add the pancetta and cook until lightly browned. Leave to cool. Beat together the eggs, milk, cream, and seasoning. Stir in the pancetta.

Spoon the pancetta mixture into the phyllo-lined molds and sprinkle with the remaining Gruyère cheese. Bake for 15 to 20 minutes until the pastry is crisp and the filling is set. Leave to cool for a few minutes on a wire rack before unmolding. Serve warm or at room temperature.

CAVIAR CANAPÉS

Blini, yeasted pancakes made with buckwheat flour, are the base of these bite-size canapés. Originally from Russia, blini are traditionally served with sour cream and caviar.

2 cups milk	2 eggs, separated
1 cup buckwheat flour	Sunflower oil, for brushing
1 tablespoon quick-rising active dry yeast	2 tablespoons butter, melted
1 teaspoon sugar	²/3 cup sour cream
³/4 cup plus 2 tablespoons all-purpose flour	4 ounces caviar or fish roe
Pinch of salt	1 tablespoon snipped fresh chives

Heat the milk in a small pan until just warm. Remove the pan from the heat. Place the buckwheat flour in a bowl and stir in the yeast and sugar. Gradually beat in half the warm milk.

Sift the all-purpose flour and salt into a separate bowl, make a well in the middle, and add the egg yolks and remaining warm milk. Beat well to make a smooth batter. Stir this mixture into the yeast mixture. Cover the bowl with plastic wrap and leave the batter to rise in a warm place until doubled in size, about 1 hour.

Beat the egg whites in a clean bowl until stiff, then fold into the batter. Heat a heavy-based skillet or griddle until hot and brush with some oil. Drop small spoonfuls of the batter onto the pan, spacing them a little apart, and cook until set and bubbles begin to appear on the surface. Turn the blini over and cook for 30 seconds longer or until golden brown. Immediately brush one side of each blin with melted butter and leave to cool on a wire rack while you make the next batch.

Once all the blini have cooled, top each one with a little sour cream and a teaspoon of caviar. Garnish with the chives and serve.

MARINATED HALLOUMI CHEESE AND TOMATO KABOBS

A Greek specialty, halloumi cheese is most frequently made from ewes' milk, although occasionally you can find a cows' milk variety. It has a salty taste and a creamy and elastic texture.

1 pound halloumi cheese	1 teaspoon crushed mixed peppercorns
24 cherry tomatoes	1 teaspoon chopped fresh oregano
2 tablespoons extra-virgin olive oil	2 teaspoons chopped fresh parsley
1 small garlic clove, crushed	Juice of ¹/2 lemon

Cut the halloumi cheese into forty-eight ¹/2-inch cubes and place in a shallow, nonmetallic dish with the cherry tomatoes. Add the oil, garlic, crushed peppercorns, oregano, parsley, and lemon juice and stir. Cover and leave to marinate in the refrigerator for at least 30 minutes or up to 24 hours.

Thread a cube of cheese onto a toothpick, then add a cherry tomato and another cube of cheese. Repeat until you assemble 24 mini kabobs. Brush them with any remaining marinade. Serve at room temperature.

PESTO PASTRY TWISTS

Instead of using pesto, try tapenade, the Mediterranean black olive paste, or chopped mixed fresh herbs. To freeze, pack the twists into a freezerproof container and freeze for up to 3 months. To serve, thaw on baking sheets, then crisp up in a 400°F oven.

4 ounces puff pastry dough, thawed if frozen
1 egg, beaten
1 tablespoon bottled pesto sauce
1/4 cup freshly grated Parmesan cheese
Freshly ground black pepper

Roll out the dough on a lightly floured board into a rectangle about 1/8 inch thick. Brush with beaten egg and spread the pesto sauce over the top. Sprinkle with the Parmesan cheese and season with pepper.

Fold the dough rectangle in half to enclose the filling and press the edges to seal well. Roll out into an 8-inch square and brush with beaten egg. Cut into 24 strips, each about 1/4 inch wide, discarding the ends. Twist each strip of dough lengthwise and arrange on a lightly oiled baking sheet, pressing the ends down flat. Chill for 15 minutes.

Meanwhile, preheat the oven to 400°F. Bake the twists for 15 minutes or until golden and puffed up. Serve warm or at room temperature.

MINI SPANAKOPITTA PURSES

Packed in a freezerproof container; these can be frozen for up to one month. To serve, spread out on a baking sheet and leave for an hour before reheating in a 350°F oven for 5 to 10 minutes.

2 pounds fresh spinach or 12 ounces frozen leaf spinach
1/2 cup butter
1 tablespoon olive oil, plus extra for greasing
1 onion, finely chopped
Good pinch of freshly grated nutmeg
24 sheets phyllo pastry dough, thawed if frozen
12 ounces feta cheese, cut into 1/2-inch cubes
Salt and freshly ground black pepper

Preheat the oven to 425°F. If the spinach is fresh, cut out any tough stems. Place it in a pan with a little boiling water and cook for 1 to 2 minutes, then drain well. If frozen, thaw it and drain well. Mix the spinach with 2 tablespoons of the butter. Heat the oil in a skillet and cook the onion until soft. Add to the spinach with the nutmeg and stir until well combined.

Cut the phyllo sheets into 8 x 4-inch rectangles, then cut in half again to make forty-eight 4-inch squares. Cover the phyllo squares with a damp dish towel when you are not working with them.

Melt the remaining butter and brush a little over one square of phyllo dough. Put another square of phyllo on top, at an angle, to make an 8-pointed star shape. Spoon a little of the spinach mixture into the middle and put a couple of pieces of feta on top. Season to taste. Bring the points of the star together so they meet in the middle, and give a twist to make a purse shape. Brush lightly with a little more melted butter. Repeat until you make 24.

Arrange the "purses" on a lightly oiled baking sheet and bake for about 15 minutes until golden brown. Serve warm or at room temperature.

SUN-DRIED TOMATO AND CHICKEN BITES WITH BASIL MAYONNAISE

These can also be made without a food processor by finely chopping the sun-dried tomatoes and olives with a knife.

7 ounces sun-dried tomatoes preserved in oil
1/2 cup pitted ripe olives
Salt and freshly ground black pepper
18 ounces boned chicken breasts, skinned
1 cup fresh white bread crumbs
2 tablespoon chopped fresh parsley
1/2 cup mayonnaise
2 tablespoons shredded fresh basil leaves
2 teaspoons bottled pesto sauce

Place the sun-dried tomatoes with the oil and the olives in a food processor and process into a rough purée. Season to taste. Cut the chicken into forty-eight 1-inch cubes and place in a shallow, nonmetallic dish. Spread the tomato and olive mixture over, cover, and leave to marinate in the refrigerator for at least 30 minutes or up to 24 hours.

Preheat the oven to 400°F. Mix together the bread crumbs, parsley, and seasoning in a small bowl. Thread 2 pieces of chicken onto each of 24 wooden toothpicks and sprinkle with the bread-crumb mixture. Arrange on a lightly oiled baking sheet and bake for about 10 minutes until the chicken is cooked through and tender.

Meanwhile, mix together the mayonnaise, basil, pesto, and seasoning in a small serving bowl. Serve the chicken hot or at room temperature, with the basil mayonnaise for dipping.

Sun-Dried Tomato and Chicken Bites with Basil Mayonnaise

27

Mini potato patties with bacon and blue cheese

These canapés literally take minutes to make. Potato patties freeze very well and are a useful standby to have in the freezer.

4 slices maple-cured slab bacon	*2 tablespoons butter, melted*
6 ounces blue cheese, such as Danish blue	*1 tablespoon chopped fresh parsley*
12 potato patties, thawed if frozen	*Freshly ground black pepper*

Preheat the broiler. Broil the bacon until crisp and golden, then snip into thin strips while still warm and set aside. Remove any rind from the cheese and cut into twenty-four 1-inch slices. Stamp out two 2-inch circles from each potato patty, using a fluted metal cutter. Place on a rack in the foil-lined broiler pan.

Toast the potato patties on one side, then turn them over and brush lightly with the butter. Top each potato patty with a slice of cheese and broil until it is just melted and bubbling. Arrange the snipped bacon on top and sprinkle with parsley. Season with pepper and serve at once.

Miniature savory choux puffs

It is important to split the cooked choux puffs as soon as they come out of the oven, to let the steam escape. Then return them to the oven so they dry completely.

3/4 cup all-purpose flour	*4 ounces sliced smoked bacon*
Salt and freshly ground black pepper	*1/2 cup garlic-and-herb flavored cream*
3 tablespoons butter	*cheese*
2 eggs, beaten	*2/3 cup heavy cream*

Preheat the oven to 375°F. Sift the flour and a good pinch of salt into a bowl. Place the butter in a pan with 2/3 cup water and heat slowly until the butter melts. Bring to a boil, then remove the pan from the heat and tip in the flour and salt.

Beat well with a wooden spoon and return the pan to the stove over low heat. Continue beating until the mixture becomes thick and leaves the sides of the pan in a ball. Remove the pan from the heat and leave to cool slightly, then gradually beat in the eggs.

Drop 24 teaspoonfuls of the mixture onto dampened baking sheets, spacing them slightly apart. Bake for about 15 minutes until well risen and golden brown. Make a small slit in the side of each puff and return to the oven for 5 minutes. Leave to cool on a wire rack.

Preheat the broiler. Broil the bacon until crisp, then snip into small pieces. Beat the cream cheese with the cream until thick and smooth. Stir in the bacon and season to taste.

Spoon the bacon filling into the choux puffs and pile into a pyramid on a serving platter.

Scones with smoked salmon and chives

Scones freeze very well. Cool the baked scones, then place them in a freezerproof container and freeze for up to one month. To serve, thaw at room temperature for 1 hour.

5 ounces smoked salmon (trimmings are fine)	*FOR THE SCONES*
1/2 cup crème fraîche	*1 3/4 cups all-purpose flour, plus extra for dusting*
2 tablespoons snipped fresh chives	*1/2 teaspoon salt*
Freshly ground black pepper	*1 teaspoon baking powder*
	3 tablespoons butter
	2/3 cup buttermilk

Preheat the oven to 425°F. To make the scones, sift the flour, salt, and baking powder into a bowl. Cut in the butter, then make a well in the middle, and add the buttermilk. Stir to make a soft dough and knead briefly on a lightly floured board.

Roll out the dough until 1/2 inch thick and stamp out 12 circles, using a 2-inch fluted cutter. Arrange slightly apart on a baking sheet dusted with flour and bake for 12 to 15 minutes until well risen and golden brown. Leave to cool on a wire rack.

Meanwhile, cut the smoked salmon into pieces. Split the scones in half and place a piece of salmon on each half. Spoon a little crème fraîche on top and sprinkle with some chives. Season with pepper and serve.

Blood sausage with apple

Don't be put off by idea of this English specialty, made with pig's blood, suet, and bread crumbs. The combination of the spiced applesauce, rich blood sausage, and toast is delicious. Contact a butcher who specializes in variety meats to locate blood sausages.

2 firm dessert apples, peeled, cored and chopped	*6 slices whole-wheat bread*
1/2 teaspoon apple pie spice	*4 slices butter, softened*
1 tablespoon heavy cream	*28 ounces blood sausage*
1 tablespoon Calvados	*Freshly ground black pepper*
	1 tablespoon chopped fresh parsley

Place the apples, apple pie spice, and 2 tablespoons water in a pan and bring to a boil. Lower the heat and simmer, stirring occasionally, until a rough purée forms. Stir in the cream and Calvados and heat through gently. Keep warm until needed.

Toast the bread. Stamp out 4 circles from each slice, using a 2-inch fluted cutter. Lightly butter the toast circles and set aside. Preheat the broiler. Cut the blood sausage into 24 slices and peel off the casing. Broil for 1 to 2 minutes on each side until just cooked through.

To serve, place a piece of blood sausage on each piece of toast and spoon some of the applesauce on top. Season with the pepper, sprinkle with the parsley, and serve at once while still hot.

Scones with Smoked Salmon and Chives

PROSCIUTTO AND ARUGULA CROSTINI

These are very simple to make and the topping can be varied endlessly. Some ideas include cubed mozzarella or Fontina cheese with sliced tomato and shredded basil, or sautéed mushrooms and walnuts sprinkled with snipped fresh chives. Each of these variations will keep in the refrigerator for up to an hour before serving.

1 thin French baguette	Salt and freshly ground black pepper
5 tablespoons extra-virgin olive oil	6 large slices prosciutto
2 ounces arugula leaves	1 ounce Parmesan cheese, cut into thin
1 tablespoon red-wine vinegar	shavings

Preheat the broiler. Cut the baguette into 24 slices, discarding the ends. Brush both sides of each slice with olive oil, using about 3 tablespoons, and broil for 8 to 10 minutes, turning over all the slices once, until golden. Leave to cool on a wire rack.

Shred any large arugula leaves. Place the arugula in a bowl. To make the dressing, put the remaining oil in a screw-top jar with the vinegar and seasoning. Shake to combine, then pour over the arugula and toss to coat all the leaves.

Top each slice of toast with a small handful of the dressed leaves. Cut each slice of prosciutto into 4 pieces and roll each one into a cigar shape. Place on top of the arugula leaves and garnish with the Parmesan shavings. Season with a little more pepper and serve.

ASPARAGUS BOREK

Borek is a Turkish term for a pastry-wrapped savory.

24 asparagus stalks	3 tablespoons freshly grated Parmesan
12 sheets phyllo pastry dough, thawed	cheese
if frozen	Salt and freshly ground black pepper
4 tablespoons butter, melted	

Preheat the oven to 400°F. Trim the asparagus stalks into 4-inch pieces, discarding the woody ends. Place in a pan of lightly salted boiling water and simmer for 2 minutes. Drain and refresh under cold running water. Pat dry with paper towels.

Cut the sheets of phyllo into twenty-four 6-inch squares and cover with a damp dish towel. Working with one phyllo square at a time, brush with melted butter and sprinkle lightly with some of the Parmesan cheese.

Place an asparagus spear at one end of the square and season with pepper. Fold in the edges and roll up into a neat cigar shape, enclosing the asparagus completely. Brush with a little more of the melted butter and place on a lightly oiled baking tray. Repeat with the remaining ingredients to make 24. Bake for 10 to 12 minutes or until lightly golden. Serve hot.

MINIATURE SALMON BALLS WITH LEMON–BUTTER SAUCE

These can be made 24 hours in advance; arranged on a baking sheet, covered, and chilled until needed. They can be frozen for up to one month: quick-freeze on a baking sheet, then pack into a container.

12 ounces potatoes, cut into chunks	2 tablespoons chopped fresh parsley
3/4 cup chicken stock	A little all-purpose flour
1/2 cup unsalted butter, diced	2 eggs, beaten
2 shallots, minced	2 1/2 cups fresh white bread crumbs
12 ounces salmon fillet, skinned	Vegetable oil, for deep-frying
Salt and freshly ground black pepper	Juice of 1 lemon
2/3 cup dry white wine	

Cook the potatoes in boiling salted water until tender, then drain and return to the heat to dry. Remove from the heat and mash; set aside. Place the stock in a small pan and boil to reduce by two-thirds.

Melt 2 tablespoons of the butter in a pan and cook the shallots until softened. Place the salmon on top, season, and add the wine and just enough water to cover. Simmer for 5 minutes or until the salmon is firm but still deep pink in the middle. Remove with a slotted spoon, leave to cool slightly, and break into flakes.

Boil the juices left in the pan until reduced to about 1 tablespoon. Pour into a bowl, add the salmon, parsley, and potatoes, and beat with a wooden spoon until well combined. Season to taste. Roll into 24 small balls, using the palms of your hands. Lightly dust with flour, then dip into the beaten egg and roll in bread crumbs.

Heat the oil to 350°F or until a cube of bread will brown in 30 seconds. Fry the salmon balls in batches for 4 to 5 minutes until golden brown. Drain on paper towels and keep warm.

Return the reduced stock to a boil. Whisk in the lemon juice and remaining butter. Pour into a bowl and serve with the salmon balls.

GRAPE LEAF BUNDLES WITH GOAT CHEESE AND OLIVES

These can also be grilled over medium-hot coals for about the same length of time, making them the perfect barbecue party canapés.

24 grape leaves in brine, drained	1/2 cup pitted ripe olives, quartered
4 tablespoons extra-virgin olive oil	Salt and freshly ground black pepper
12 ounces goat cheese	

Rinse the grape leaves under cold running water, pat dry with paper towels, and brush one side of each with oil, using about half of the oil.

Cut the goat cheese into 24 pieces. Place a piece of cheese and a few olive quarters on each grape leaf. Season well, then roll up the leaves to enclose the filling completely. Secure each bundle with a toothpick. Brush the bundles with the remaining oil.

Preheat the broiler. Broil the bundles for 2 to 3 minutes on each side until lightly charred. Serve warm.

Prosciutto and Arugula Crostini

FRENCH-STYLE STUFFED MUSSELS

When buying fresh mussels, it is important that their shells are tightly closed, or that any open ones close if you tap them. This indicates that the mussels are alive and fresh. Discard any that do not close.

24 large live mussels
²/₃ cup dry white wine
2 shallots, minced
Juice of ¹/₂ lemon
6 tablespoons butter

2 garlic cloves, crushed
2 cups fresh white bread crumbs
2 tablespoons chopped fresh parsley
Salt and freshly ground black pepper

Scrub the mussels, remove the beards, and rinse well in cold water. Place them in a large pan with the wine and shallots, cover, and cook over high heat for about 5 minutes until all the mussels open, shaking the pan frequently. Discard any that do not open. Drain the mussels and remove all the empty half shells. Arrange the mussels in their half shells on the foil-lined broiler rack and sprinkle with lemon juice.

Preheat the broiler. Melt the butter in a small pan and sauté the garlic for 20 seconds. Remove from the heat and stir in the bread crumbs, parsley, and seasoning. Sprinkle a little of this mixture over each mussel and broil for 1 to 2 minutes until light brown. Serve hot.

TOASTED POLENTA FINGERS WITH DOLCELATTE SAUCE

This sauce should be served warm, ideally in a small fondue pot or a bowl on a heated serving tray.

1¹/₄ cups quick-cooking polenta or yellow cornmeal
Salt and freshly ground black pepper
4 tablespoons butter

FOR THE DOLCELATTE SAUCE
1 garlic clove, halved
2 teaspoons cornstarch
2 tablespoons lemon juice
6 tablespoons dry white wine
8 ounces dolcelatte cheese, rind removed

Bring 5 cups cold water to a boil in a large saucepan. Add 1 teaspoon salt and pour in the polenta or cornmeal in a continuous, thin stream, stirring with a wooden spoon. Simmer for about 15 minutes until the mixture is thick and no longer grainy, stirring occasionally.

Remove the pan from the heat and stir in half the butter. Season with pepper. Turn out onto a board and spread out until ¹/₂ inch thick. Leave to cool, then cover and chill for at least 1 hour.

Preheat the broiler. Cut the set polenta into 24 diamond shapes, each about 1¹/₂ inches long, and place on the foil-lined broiler rack. Melt the remaining butter and brush over both sides of the polenta shapes. Broil for 3 to 4 minutes on each side. Cover loosely and keep warm.

To make the sauce, rub the garlic around the inside of a small heavy-based pan, then discard the garlic. Blend the cornstarch to a paste with the lemon juice. Put the wine in the pan with the blended cornstarch, crumble in the dolcelatte cheese, and slowly bring to a boil, stirring constantly. Simmer for 5 minutes, stirring frequently. Season with pepper. Serve warm, with the toasted polenta fingers for dipping.

CHEESE AND OLIVE SABLÉ SHAPES

Instead of the olives, garnish these crackers with chopped sun-dried tomatoes that have been preserved in oil, or small pieces of anchovy fillet. They can be frozen for up to a month. To serve, thaw, then put them on baking sheets in a 400°F oven until crisp. Makes about 20.

10 small pitted ripe olives, halved

FOR THE DOUGH
¹/₂ cup plus 2 tablespoons all-purpose flour, plus extra for dusting
4 tablespoons chilled butter, cubed

¹/₂ cup freshly grated Parmesan cheese
1 egg, beaten

Preheat the oven to 350°F. Sift the flour into a bowl and cut in the butter until the mixture resembles fine bread crumbs. Stir in the cheese with 1 tablespoon chilled water and mix to make a firm dough.

Knead the dough briefly and roll out thinly on a lightly floured board. Stamp out 20 star and moon shapes and arrange on a baking sheet. Brush with the beaten egg and press half an olive into the middle of each one. Bake for 10 to 12 minutes until crisp and golden brown. Leave to cool on a wire rack before serving.

CHICKEN LIVER PÂTÉ TOASTS WITH ONION CONSERVE

The quantity of pâté in this recipe is greater than in the other recipes in the chapter because less will not blend properly in most food processors. The pâté and conserve can be made up to 24 hours in advance and chilled until needed. Makes 48.

2 tablespoons unsalted butter
8 ounces chicken livers, thawed if frozen
1 small garlic clove, crushed
¹/₂ teaspoon chopped fresh marjoram
2 tablespoons brandy
12 slices white bread

FOR THE ONION CONSERVE
2 tablespoons butter
2 onions, thinly sliced
2 tablespoons sugar
3 tablespoons red currant jelly
2 tablespoons red-wine vinegar
²/₃ cup red wine
Salt and freshly ground black pepper

Melt half the butter in a pan and gently cook the chicken livers, garlic, and marjoram for about 10 minutes, stirring occasionally. Stir in the brandy and remove from the heat. Leave to cool slightly. Place the mixture in a food processor and blend until smooth. Spoon into a small dish and chill for at least 2 hours until firm.

To make the onion conserve, melt the butter in a pan, add the onions, and cook over low heat, uncovered, for about 30 minutes, stirring frequently. Add the sugar, red currant jelly, vinegar, and wine and cook slowly for 20 minutes longer or until thickened. Season to taste.

Toast the bread and stamp out 4 circles from each slice, using a 2-inch metal cutter. Leave to cool on a wire rack.

To serve, spread each piece of toast thickly with some of the chicken liver pâté and place a little of the onion conserve on top.

QUICK & EASY

Very few people have the time to spend hours in the kitchen preparing food. The recipes in this chapter have been devised with the busy cook in mind. Each can be made in less than half an hour, and the number of necessary ingredients have been kept to a minimum. Many of the dishes can be made simply using ingredients for a well-stocked cupboard. Just follow the suggestions for useful ingredients on pages 9 to 11, stocking the ones you consider most useful. All recipes serve 4.

CORN FRITTERS WITH SWEET CHILI SAUCE

Many flavorings, such as crushed garlic and ginger or finely chopped red chili, can be added to the batter. But these fritters also taste wonderful just as they are, dipped into a little sweet chili sauce.

1 can (7-ounce) corn kernels, drained	*1 egg*
3 tablespoons all-purpose flour	*Salt and freshly ground black pepper*
1 teaspoon baking powder	*Vegetable oil, for frying*
1 teaspoon hot chili powder	*¹/₂ cup bottled sweet chili sauce*

Place the corn, flour, baking powder, chili powder, and egg in a bowl and stir until combined. Season generously.

Heat 1 inch oil in a deep skillet. Put 5 or 6 heaped tablespoons of the batter into the pan and flatten slightly with a fork. Fry for about 5 minutes, turning once, until crisp and golden brown. Drain on paper towels. Keep each batch warm while frying the remainder. Serve hot, with the chili sauce.

FRITTO MISTO

Cod, haddock, and sole are ideal white fish fillets to use in this recipe, and ¹/₄-inch squid rings are also suitable.

8 ounces firm white fish fillets, skinned	*2 tablespoons seasoned flour*
4 small red mullets, dressed and filleted	*Vegetable oil, for deep-frying*
12 raw jumbo shrimp or tiger prawns	*Lemon wedges, to garnish*

Cut the white fish fillets into long, thin strips, and slice the red mullet fillets. Shell the shrimp, leaving the shells on their tails. Place the seasoned flour on a plate and toss all the seafood in flour to coat.

Heat the oil to 375°F or until a cube of bread will brown in 20 seconds. Add the seafood pieces a few at a time and fry until golden brown. Drain on paper towels. Keep each batch warm while frying the remainder. Arrange on a serving platter, garnish with the lemon wedges, and serve.

GARLIC PITA FINGERS WITH TARAMASALATA

Look for taramasalata, a pale pink dip made with smoked cod or other fish roe, at the supermarket delicatessen counter. Popular in Greece, it is enjoyed drizzled with olive oil and with plenty of pita bread for scooping it up. Pita bread is a good standby to have in the freezer because it can be broiled from frozen.

4 tablespoons butter	*Salt and freshly ground black pepper*
2 garlic cloves, crushed	*8 white pita breads*
1 tablespoon chopped fresh herbs, such as oregano and parsley	*²/₃ cup taramasalata*

Preheat the broiler. Melt the butter in a small pan and stir in the garlic, herbs, and seasoning. Arrange the pita breads on the broiler rack and broiler for 1 minute.

Turn the pita breads over and brush liberally with the garlic butter. Broil for 1 to 2 minutes longer, then cut into strips. Serve at once with the taramasalata.

Melted Cheese and Corn Nachos

SWEET POTATO STICKS WITH BLUE CHEESE DIP

The crisp Parmesan cheese coating on these sticks, like french fries, is perfectly complemented by the blue cheese and yogurt dip.

1 pound sweet potatoes
1 tablespoon seasoned flour
1 egg
Salt and freshly ground black pepper
3/4 cup dried white bread crumbs

1/4 cup freshly grated Parmesan cheese
Sunflower oil, for deep-frying
3/4 cup crumbled soft blue cheese
4 tablespoons thick plain yogurt

Peel the sweet potatoes and cut them into sticks. Coat in the seasoned flour. Beat the egg with 2 tablespoons water and season well. Combine the bread crumbs, Parmesan cheese, and seasoning on a plate. Coat the sweet potato sticks in the beaten egg and then in the bread crumb mixture.

Heat the oil to 350°F or until a cube of bread will brown in 30 seconds. While the oil is heating, mash the blue cheese in a small bowl and gradually beat in the yogurt. Season to taste and set aside.

Fry the sweet potato sticks in batches for 3 to 4 minutes until crisp and golden. Drain on paper towels and serve at once, with the dip.

SAUSAGE AND HERB NUGGETS WITH APRICOT RELISH

Buy good-quality sausage meat that is not too fatty for this recipe. You can use any combination of herbs you like—parsley, sage, and thyme are classic flavorings with pork sausages.

1 can (16-ounce) apricot halves in syrup
3 tablespoons sunflower oil
1 onion, finely chopped
2 tablespoons white-wine vinegar
2 teaspoons black mustard seed

1 pound fresh sausage meat
2 tablespoons chopped fresh herbs, such as thyme, sage, and parsley
2 tablespoons seasoned flour

To make the apricot relish, drain the apricots, reserving 6 tablespoons of the juice. Chop the apricots into small pieces. Heat 1 tablespoon of the oil in a pan and cook the onion until softened. Add the apricots, reserved juice, vinegar, and mustard seed and simmer for about 15 minutes until reduced and thicker.

Knead the sausage meat with the herbs and 4 tablespoons of the apricot relish. Divide into 20 pieces and roll each into a ball with wet hands. Dust the balls lightly with the seasoned flour.

Heat the remaining oil in a large skillet and cook the sausage nuggets for about 10 minutes until lightly golden, turning them over occasionally. Drain on paper towels and place on a serving platter. Serve hot, with the rest of the apricot relish in a small bowl for dipping.

MELTED CHEESE AND CORN NACHOS

This literally takes minutes to make. Thawed frozen corn kernels, as well as the canned variety, can also be used. Or, if fresh corn is in season, scrape the kernels off the cob and cook them in a little water for about 5 minutes until just they are just tender.

8 ounces tortilla chips
1/2 cup corn kernels, drained if necessry
2 tomatoes, chopped
4 scallions, chopped

4 tablespoons sour cream
Salt and freshly ground black pepper
1/2 cup grated Cheddar cheese

Preheat the broiler. Spread the tortilla chips in a large, shallow flameproof dish and scatter with the corn kernels, tomatoes, and scallions. Spoon the sour cream over, season to taste, and sprinkle with the Cheddar cheese.

Broil for 2 to 3 minutes until the cheese melts and is bubbling. Serve at once.

QUICK MOZZARELLA AND SALAMI PIZZAS

To make this recipe even quicker, use 1 cup canned or bottled tomato sauce with herbs for the base and skip the first step.

3 tablespoons olive oil	*Salt and freshly ground black pepper*
1 small onion, finely chopped	*4 English muffins*
1 can (14-ounce) crushed tomatoes	*5 ounces salami, sliced*
1 tablespoon tomato paste	*8 ounces mozzarella cheese, sliced*
1 teaspoon Italian seasoning	

Heat half the oil in a small pan and sauté the onion until soft. Stir in the tomatoes, tomato paste, Italian seasoning, and salt and pepper, and simmer for 5 to 10 minutes until reduced and thicker.

Preheat the broiler. Split the muffins in half horizontally and spread some of the tomato mixture on the rough surface of each half. Cut the salami slices into quarters, if large, and scatter over the muffin halves. Arrange the mozzarella on top and drizzle with the remaining oil. Broil for about 5 minutes until bubbling and golden. Serve at once.

FRIED EGGPLANT WITH SKORDALIA

This traditional Greek dish is often served as part of a *mezze* (a selection of appetizers) in restaurants. Serve it as soon as all the eggplant slices are fried or they will start to become soft.

olive oil, for frying
1 pound eggplant, thinly sliced
2 tablespoons seasoned flour

FOR THE SKORDALIA

1 cup day-old white bread crumbs	*1 tablespoon white-wine vinegar*
3/4 cup milk	*2/3 cup extra-virgin olive oil*
2 garlic cloves, crushed	*Salt and freshly ground black pepper*

To make the skordalia, place the bread crumbs and milk in a bowl and leave to soak for 10 minutes. Whisk in the garlic and vinegar, then slowly pour in the olive oil in a thin, steady stream, whisking constantly. Season to taste and set aside.

Preheat the oven to its lowest setting. Pour 1/2 inch of olive oil into a deep skillet and heat to 375°F or until a cube of bread will brown in 20 seconds. Dip the eggplant slices in the seasoned flour and fry in batches for 1 to 2 minutes until golden brown. Drain on paper towels and keep warm in the oven while frying the remainder.

Arrange the fried eggplant on serving plates with the skordalia on the side and serve at once.

CRISPY MUSHROOMS WITH GOAT CHEESE DIP

Goat cheese is available in a variety of textures, from solid logs that can be sliced to soft cheese that is so creamy it must be spread on bread or a cracker to be eaten. For this recipe, you want the creamy variety. Look for it in supermarkets, gourmet stores, and delicatessens.

8 ounces soft goat cheese	*2 eggs*
4 tablespoons sour cream	*Salt and freshly ground black pepper*
2 tablespoons snipped fresh chives	*3/4 cup dried bread crumbs*
1 pound mixed mushrooms, such as	*Vegetable oil, for deep-frying*
cremini, button, or wild	*1 tablespoon lemon juice*

Place the goat cheese in a bowl and beat with a wooden spoon until smooth. Beat in the sour cream and chives until well combined. Taste and add a little seasoning if necessary, then spoon into a small serving bowl. Cover and chill if not serving immediately.

Cut the large mushrooms into bite-sized pieces; smaller ones can be left whole. Beat the eggs in a bowl and season well. Dip the mushrooms first into the beaten egg and then into the bread crumbs to coat completely.

Heat the oil to 350°F or until a cube of bread will brown in 30 seconds. Fry the mushrooms in batches for 1 to 2 minutes until crisp and golden. Drain on paper towels, sprinkle with lemon juice, and serve at once, with the goat cheese dip.

Quick Mozzarella and Salami Pizzas

CRISPY NEW POTATOES WITH MUSTARD RELISH

These bacon-wrapped potatoes are delicious on their own, but the mustard-flavored relish is an excellent extra. Look for it in the condiment section of your supermarket.

20 baby new potatoes
10 slices smoked bacon
3 tablespoons olive oil
1 tablespoon chopped fresh thyme

2 garlic cloves, finely chopped
Salt and freshly ground black pepper
3/4 cup bottled mustard relish

Preheat the oven to 400°F. Place the potatoes in a pan of boiling salted water and cook for 10 to 15 minutes until just tender. Meanwhile, cut each bacon slice in half lengthwise. Place the oil, thyme, garlic, and seasoning in a bowl.

When the potatoes are tender, drain and tip them into the oil mixture, stirring to coat. Wrap a piece of bacon around each potato and place them in a single layer in a small roasting pan. Drizzle with the remaining oil mixture and bake for 15 to 20 minutes until crisp. Serve the potatoes hot, with the mustard relish as a dip.

MOZZARELLA FRITTERS WITH SPICY TOMATO SAUCE

Traditional Italian mozzarella is creamy white and usually sold in balls. The Danish version, however, is slightly yellow and comes in block form, making it easier to slice. Look for this at specialist cheese stores and delicatessens.

1 can (14-ounce) crushed tomatoes
4 tablespoons bottled sweet chili sauce
1/2 teaspoon cayenne pepper
Salt and freshly ground black pepper
12 ounces Danish mozzarella cheese

2 cups fine fresh white bread crumbs
2 tablespoons chopped fresh parsley
2 eggs
Vegetable oil, for deep-frying

Place the tomatoes, chili sauce, half the cayenne, and a little seasoning in a small pan. Bring to a boil, then reduce the heat and simmer for 15 to 20 minutes until well reduced and thicker.

Meanwhile, cut the mozzarella cheese into twelve 1 x 3-inch slices. Mix together the bread crumbs, parsley, remaining cayenne pepper, and seasoning in a bowl. Lightly beat the eggs in a small bowl. Dip the mozzarella slices first into the beaten egg and then into the bread crumb mixture. Repeat the process, dipping them carefully the second time so the first layer of coating doesn't fall off.

Heat the oil to 375°F or until a cube of bread will brown in 20 seconds. Deep-fry the mozzarella slices in batches for about 2 minutes until crisp and golden. Drain on paper towels and serve hot, with the warm sauce.

BAGNA CAUDA

This full-flavored garlic and anchovy dip can be eaten with a seemingly endless selection of raw vegetables—instead of carrots and radishes, try cauliflower or broccoli florets, sliced bell peppers or zucchini sticks. Keep the dip warm while you serve it over a food warmer with a candle or in a fondue pot.

4 tablespoons unsalted butter
1/2 cup extra-virgin olive oil
2 large garlic cloves, crushed
1 can (2-ounce) anchovy fillets, drained
Freshly ground black pepper

2 large carrots, cut into sticks
4 ounces radishes
8 ounces Italian-style bread, cut into chunks

Melt the butter in a pan with the oil and stir in the garlic and anchovies. Cook over very low heat for 10 to 15 minutes, stirring frequently, until the anchovies dissolve. Season with pepper.

Serve warm with the vegetables and bread for dipping.

Crispy New Potatoes with Mustard Relish

SWISS CHEESE FONDUE

You can make this even if you don't have a fondue pot. Place the saucepan you use to make the creamy cheese sauce over a food warmer with a lit candle and let everyone dip their bread into the pan.

1 large garlic clove, halved
2 teaspoons cornstarch
2 tablespoons kirsch
2 cups grated Swiss cheese

1 cup grated Gruyère cheese
1 cup dry white wine
Freshly ground black pepper
1 large French baguette, cut into chunks

Rub the inside of a fondue pan or small heavy-based saucepan with the cut surface of the garlic; discard the garlic. Blend the cornstarch to a paste with the kirsch and place in the pot or pan with the cheeses and wine. Bring slowly to a boil, stirring continuously.

Lower the heat and simmer for 3 to 4 minutes, stirring frequently. Season to taste with the pepper. Place the pot or pan over a fondue burner or food warmer at the table. Serve with the bread for dipping.

VEGETABLE CHIPS WITH SOUR CREAM DIP

These fried vegetable slices have become very fashionable and are served in some of the best restaurants. They taste wonderful and make a much more colorful snack than everyday potato chips.

1 parsnip
1 large carrot
1 cooked beet
Vegetable oil, for frying

2/3 cup sour cream
2 tablespoons snipped fresh chives
Salt and freshly ground black pepper

Using a vegetable peeler or sharp knife, cut the vegetables into very thin slices. Pat with paper towels to remove any excess moisture.

Heat about 1 inch of oil in a deep skillet and fry the vegetables in batches for 1 to 2 minutes until golden. Remove them with a slotted spoon and drain on paper towels. When all the vegetables have been fried, season well and arrange them on a serving platter.

Mix together the sour cream and chives. Season to taste and serve in a small bowl, with the vegetable chips.

SPANISH OMELET WEDGES

Use a skillet with a flameproof handle, such as cast iron, so it doesn't burn under the broiler. If, however, your skillet has a wooden or plastic handle, wrap it with a double thickness of foil for protection.

4 tablespoons olive oil
1 3/4 cups sliced onions
3 cups thinly sliced potatoes
8 ounces young, tender leaf spinach, thawed if frozen

1/2 cup grated Gruyère cheese
6 eggs
Salt and freshly ground black pepper

Heat the oil in an 8-inch flameproof skillet and cook the onions for about 10 minutes until soft. Meanwhile, blanch the potato slices in a pan of boiling salted water for 3 minutes. Drain and pat dry.

Add the potatoes to the pan with the onions and cook for 5 minutes longer or until the potatoes are light golden, stirring frequently. Stir in the spinach leaves and cook for 1 to 2 minutes longer until just wilted. Sprinkle the cheese on top.

Preheat the broiler. Beat the eggs in a bowl with plenty of seasoning, then pour over the potato and onion mixture, pressing down gently with the back of a wooden spoon or spatula. Cook for 5 minutes or until the top is nearly set. Transfer to the hot broiler and broil for 2 to 3 minutes until set and golden brown. Cut into 8 wedges and serve hot, warm, or at room temperature.

SIZZLING CHORIZO AND CHERRY TOMATO KABOBS

A mixture of red and yellow cherry tomatoes looks very attractive but a totally red selection is just as suitable. Chorizo is a spicy Spanish or Mexican pork sausage. It gets it hotness and distinctive bright red color from paprika. If sun-dried tomato paste is unavailable, purée sun-dried tomatoes preserved in oil in a food processor or blender until a thick paste forms.

3 tablespoons sun-dried tomato paste
1 garlic clove, crushed
1/2 teaspoon chili powder

1 tablespoon honey
12 ounces chorizo sausage, sliced
8 ounces cherry tomatoes

Preheat the broiler. In a small bowl, mix together the sun-dried tomato paste, garlic, chili powder, and honey to make a thick paste. Thread the slices of chorizo and cherry tomatoes alternately onto eight 6-inch bamboo skewers.

Using a pastry brush, spread the sun-dried tomato mixture all over the kabobs, coating each one thickly. Broil for 1 to 2 minutes on each side until the sausage is cooked through and sizzling. Serve at once.

STEAMED BABY VEGETABLES WITH HOLLANDAISE SAUCE

This recipe is a chance to use the many hybrid baby vegetables, grown specifically for their miniature size and sweet, delicate flavors.

2 whole eggs plus 1 egg yolk
1 tablespoon lemon juice
Good pinch of salt
1 cup unsalted butter

1 pound mixed baby vegetables, such as carrots, corn, leeks, snow peas, and zucchini
1 tablespoon chopped fresh tarragon

Put the eggs and egg yolk, lemon juice, and salt into a food processor and blend for 10 seconds. Melt the butter in a small pan until it just begins to foam, but not burn. Then, with the food processor running, pour the butter onto the egg mixture in a steady, thin stream. Pour the sauce into the pan and heat gently, stirring frequently, for about 30 seconds until thickened. This hollandaise sauce will keep for 10 minutes without separating if you put it in a bowl set over a pan of simmering water.

Steam the baby vegetables for 4 to 5 minutes until just tender. Pour the hollandaise sauce into a bowl, stir in the tarragon, and place in the middle of a warmed serving platter. Arrange the vegetables around it and serve at once.

ZUCCHINI FRITTERS WITH RED PESTO SAUCE

Red pesto sauce, which gets its color from sun-dried tomatoes, will be available in gourmet and Italian food stores. If you can't find any, use the more traditional green pesto sauce made with basil.

1 cup all-purpose flour
Salt and freshly ground black pepper
2 eggs, separated
3/4 cup plus 2 tablespoons beer
2 tablespoons vegetable oil, plus extra for deep-frying

1 can (7-ounce) crushed tomatoes
4 tablespoons red pesto sauce
1 pound small zucchini, cut into thick slices

To make the batter, sift the flour and 1 teaspoon of salt into a bowl and make a well in the middle. Gradually beat in the egg yolks, beer, 2 tablespoons vegetable oil, and seasoning to make a smooth batter.

Stir the tomatoes and pesto sauce together in a small pan over medium heat. Season to taste and simmer for about 5 minutes until slightly thicker. Keep warm.

Heat the oil to 350°F or until a cube of bread will brown in 30 seconds. Beat the egg whites until stiff and fold them into the batter. Dip the zucchini slices into the batter a few at a time and fry in batches for 2 to 3 minutes until crisp and golden. Drain on paper towels and keep warm while frying the remainder. Serve hot, with the sauce for dipping.

BROILED SQUID WITH FETA

Squid has the undeserved reputation of being tough and rubbery. It is perfectly tender if it is cooked very quickly, as in this recipe, or very slowly. If using dressed squid, available from large supermarkets' fish counters, start with the third step of this recipe.

8 small squid, about 1 pound in total
4 tablespoons extra-virgin olive oil
2 tablespoons lemon juice
1 garlic clove, crushed

2 teaspoons chopped fresh flat-leaf parsley
Salt and freshly ground black pepper
6 ounces feta cheese, cubed

To prepare the squid, hold the body firmly in one hand, grip the head and tentacles with the other hand, and pull gently; they will come away along with the contents of the body sac.

Cut off the tentacles, just in front of the eyes, and remove the ink sac. Peel off the thin layer of skin that covers the body and discard. Pull out the transparent quill. Rinse the squid well under cold running water.

Mix together the olive oil, lemon juice, garlic, parsley, and seasoning in a shallow nonmetallic dish. Add the squid and feta and stir to coat. Set aside for 15 minutes.

Preheat the broiler. Remove the squid from the marinade and stuff each cavity with feta cheese mixture. Arrange the stuffed squid on a rack over the foil-lined broiler pan and brush with any remaining marinade. Broil for 5 minutes on each side or until cooked through and light brown. Serve hot.

GARLIC AND LEMON MUSHROOMS

Field mushrooms always have a more pronounced flavor than the cultivated variety because they have been left to mature for longer before they are picked. Some cooks peel off the skins, but unless they are very ragged or bruised, it isn't necessary.

8 large open-cap mushrooms, each about 4 inches across
2 large garlic cloves, crushed
Grated peel and juice of 1 lemon

6 tablespoons olive oil
Salt and freshly ground black pepper
2 tablespoons chopped fresh flat-leaf parsley
Warm French baguette, sliced, to serve

Preheat the oven to 400°F. Trim the stems off the mushrooms. Arrange the mushroom caps, stem side up, in a shallow roasting pan.

Mix together the garlic, lemon peel and juice, oil, and seasoning in a small bowl. Drizzle the oil mixture over the mushrooms and bake for 15 minutes. Turn the mushrooms over, baste well with the oil mixture in the pan, and bake for 5 to 10 minutes longer until tender.

Arrange the mushrooms on serving plates, scatter with parsley, and serve at once, with French bread to mop up all the juices.

Steamed Baby Vegetables with Hollandaise Sauce

LIGHT & HEALTHY

Contrary to popular belief, casual eating does not have to be unhealthy. This selection of recipes proves this point perfectly. After a late evening out, for example, a full-scale dinner is often out of the question, but a light and wholesome snack can just fit the bill. There are also a number of choices for entertaining in this chapter.

TURKEY AND CHERRY TOMATO TWISTS

Enjoying turkey doesn't have to be reserved just for Thanksgiving or Christmas. It is a low-fat meat, which makes it ideal for healthy snacking. Makes 24.

3 tablespoons plain yogurt
1 small garlic clove, crushed
1 teaspoon grated fresh gingerroot
Grated peel of 1 lime

1 tablespoon honey
Salt and freshly ground black pepper
1 pound turkey breast fillets, skinned
6 ounces tiny cherry tomatoes

Place the yogurt, garlic, ginger, lime peel, honey, and seasoning in a nonmetallic bowl. Slice the turkey into twenty-four 6 x ½-inch strips. Place in the marinade and stir to coat. Cover and chill for at least 30 minutes or overnight.

Preheat the broiler. Thread each turkey strip onto a 6-inch bamboo skewer, interweaving with the cherry tomatoes. Broil for 8 to 10 minutes, turning the skewers over occasionally, until the turkey is cooked through and tender. Serve hot.

ASPARAGUS WITH CRAB DIP

Fresh crab is ideal for this recipe, but the results will be just as tasty if you use canned or frozen crabmeat. Just take care to drain it well before you combine it with the other dip ingredients. Serves 4 to 6.

1½ pounds asparagus stalks

FOR THE CRAB DIP
8 ounces white crabmeat, flaked
2 tablespoons butter, melted
½ cup cream cheese
4 tablespoons plain yogurt

Juice of ½ lemon
2 tablespoons snipped fresh chives
Freshly ground black pepper

Trim any woody ends from the asparagus and discard. Trim all the stalks to the same length and divide into 4 equal bundles. Secure each bundle with string under the tips and near the base.

Stand the bundles in an asparagus steamer or deep saucepan. Add enough boiling salted water to come halfway up the stalks. Bring to a boil, then cover with a lid or dome of foil and simmer for 8 to 10 minutes until the bases of the stalks are just tender when pierced with a knife.

Meanwhile, to make the dip, mix all the ingredients together in a bowl with a fork or in a food processor. Pour the mixture into a serving dish.

Drain the cooked asparagus thoroughly, remove the string, and arrange on a serving platter with the dip. Serve at once while still hot.

PERSIAN BROILED BABY EGGPLANT

If you can't find baby eggplants, use three medium-sized ones and cut them lengthwise into slices. Serves 4.

½ cup coconut milk
2 garlic cloves, crushed
1 red chili, seeded and finely chopped
Grated peel of 1 small lemon

1 teaspoon ground cumin
2 tablespoons chopped fresh cilantro
10 baby eggplants
1 teaspoon salt

Place the coconut milk in a small pan and stir in the garlic, chili, lemon peel, cumin, and cilantro. Simmer for 5 to 10 minutes until a thick paste forms. Remove from the heat and leave to cool.

Meanwhile, halve the eggplants and sprinkle with the salt. Leave in a colander to drain for 30 minutes, then rinse under cold running water and pat dry with paper towels.

Preheat the broiler. Spread the coconut paste all over the cut surfaces of the eggplant halves and broil for 15 to 20 minutes until cooked through and lightly charred. Serve at once.

FALAFEL WITH YOGURT–MINT RELISH

This Middle Eastern recipe is normally deep-fried. However, it is just as successful shallow-fried so it uses less fat. Makes 24.

1 can (14-ounce) chickpeas, drained and rinsed
1 large garlic clove, crushed
½ teaspoon each ground coriander and cumin
1 egg yolk
1 cup fresh white bread crumbs
2 tablespoons olive oil

FOR THE YOGURT-MINT RELISH
⅔ cup thick plain yogurt
½ cup grated and squeezed cucumber
1 teaspoon mint sauce

To make the relish, mix together the yogurt, cucumber, and mint sauce in a small bowl. Cover and chill until needed.

Place the chickpeas, garlic, spices, and egg yolk in a food processor and blend until smooth. Stir in the bread crumbs.

Divide the falafel mixture into 24 pieces. Roll into balls and flatten slightly. Heat the olive oil in a heavy-based skillet, add the falafel, and fry for 6 to 8 minutes until golden brown all over. Serve at once, with the yogurt-mint relish for dipping.

Honey-Glazed Chicken Tikka Mini Kabobs

JUMBO SHRIMP WITH TRICOLOR DIP

For special occasions, use Dublin Bay prawns or langoustines from specialist fish merchants. Both crustaceans look like a cross between shrimp and lobster, and have a sweet, delicate flavor. Makes 24.

24 fresh raw jumbo shrimp

FOR THE TRICOLOR DIP

1 large orange bell pepper, seeded and	*1 small garlic clove, crushed*
quartered	*1–2 teaspoons lemon juice*
6 tablespoons thick plain yoghurt	*Salt and freshly ground black pepper*
2 tablespoons sour cream	*2 teaspoons snipped fresh chives*

Rinse the shrimp in cold water. Place them in a large pan of boiling water, return to a boil, and poach for 3 minutes. Drain, refresh quickly under cold running water, and leave to cool. Shell the shrimp, leaving the tail shells on.

To make the dip, preheat the broiler. Broil the pepper until the skin is charred. Wrap in plastic wrap and leave to cool, then peel off the skin. Purée the pepper flesh in a food processor or blender.

Meanwhile, put the yogurt, sour cream, garlic, lemon juice, and seasoning in a bowl and stir well. Spoon into a serving bowl and swirl in the pepper purée, using a thin metal skewer. Sprinkle the chives in a small heap in the middle of the dip, and serve with the shrimp.

HONEY-GLAZED CHICKEN TIKKA MINI KABOBS

Curry paste, sold in jars in the foreign food section of supermarkets and Asian food stores, adds a spicy, Indian-style flavor to dishes without having to first cook off the "raw" taste of numerous spices. Tikka-flavored curries are instantly recognized by their bright orange color. Makes 24.

1 pound boneless chicken breast, skinned	*1 tablespoon bottled tikka curry paste*
4 tablespoons plain yogurt	*3 tablespoons honey*
2 garlic cloves, crushed	*1 tablespoon lemon juice*
1-inch piece fresh gingerroot, crushed	*1 tablespoon finely chopped fresh mint*
1/2 teaspoon salt	

Cut the chicken into 1/2-inch cubes. Mix together the yogurt, garlic, ginger, salt, and curry paste in a bowl. Stir in the chicken cubes and leave them to marinate for at least 30 minutes or up to 12 hours.

Preheat the broiler. Thread the marinated chicken onto 24 toothpicks and broil for 2 to 3 minutes on each side.

Meanwhile, warm the honey and lemon juice together in a small pan. Brush all over each mini kabob, sprinkle with mint, and serve at once.

POTATO SKINS WITH AVOCADO AND RED ONION SALSA

To prepare this in advance, brush the potato skins with oil and make the salsa, then cover both and chill for up to 24 hours. When ready to serve, bake the potato skins in a preheated 400°F oven for about 15 minutes until golden. Serves 4.

6 potatoes, about 4 ounces each
2 tablespoons sunflower oil

FOR THE AVOCADO AND RED ONION SALSA

1 1/2 cups diced ripe tomatoes	*2 tablespoons bottled chili sauce*
1 ripe avocado, diced	*Salt and freshly ground black pepper*
1 small red onion, minced	

Preheat the oven to 400°F. Scrub the potatoes and dry them well with paper towels. Rub each potato with a little of the oil and place them directly on the oven shelf. Bake for 40 to 45 minutes until they are slightly soft when squeezed.

Meanwhile, make the salsa. Mix together the tomatoes, avocado, onion, and chili sauce in a small bowl. Season to taste. Cover with plastic wrap and chill until needed.

When the potatoes are tender, remove them from the oven and cut them in half lengthwise and then into quarters. Slice away some of the flesh, leaving a layer of potato at least 1/2 inch thick on the skin.

Preheat the broiler. Spread the potato skins on baking sheets, brush lightly with the remaining oil, and broil for 5 to 10 minutes until crisp and golden brown. Arrange the potato skins on a serving plate with the salsa, sprinkle with a little salt, and serve.

MARINATED GREEK OLIVES

Although these olives are preserved in oil, once they are drained there is hardly any oil left on them. They can also be used in cocktails. Makes 3 to 4 cups.

1 pound large green olives
4 small garlic cloves, peeled
Pared peel of 1 lemon
6 small dried red chilies

2 sprigs each fresh thyme and oregano
1 teaspoon fennel seeds
Olive oil, for filling

Using the tip of a sharp knife, cut a slit in each olive through to the pit. Layer the olives with the garlic, lemon peel, chilies, herb sprigs, and fennel seeds in a glass jar.

Pour in enough oil to cover the olives completely, then close the jar and leave for at least one week or up to one month before using.

TABBOULEH PARTY PITA POCKETS

These make the perfect calorie-conscious canapés. You can also use the mixture to stuff warmed mini pita breads for a healthy snack. Makes 24.

2/3 cup bulgur wheat
Juice of 1 large lemon
1 small garlic clove, crushed
2 tablespoons each chopped fresh mint and parsley

1/2 teaspoon ground cumin
2 tomatoes, peeled, seeded, and diced
4 scallions, minced
4 ounces feta cheese, finely diced
24 mini pita breads

Soak the bulgur wheat in a large bowl of cold water for 30 minutes; drain thoroughly. Blend the lemon juice, garlic, mint, parsley, and cumin in a small bowl and stir into the bulgur wheat. Leave to marinate for at least 30 minutes and up to 8 hours.

Add the tomatoes, scallions, and feta cheese and mix well.

Lightly toast the mini pita breads and split each one across the top. Stuff with the tabbouleh and serve.

MIXED MUSHROOM BASKETS

It is important not to let the fromage frais come to a boil or it will curdle and separate. Serves 4.

4 round white rolls
3 tablespoons butter
1 onion, minced
10 ounces mixed mushrooms, such as oyster, shiitake, and cremini, sliced if large

1 tablespoon Madeira wine
6 tablespoons low-fat fromage frais
2 teaspoons snipped fresh chives
Salt and freshly ground black pepper

Preheat the oven to 400°F. Cut the tops off the rolls and scoop out the middles, leaving a 1/2-inch shell. Melt half the butter and brush inside the rolls. Bake for 8 to 10 minutes until golden.

Melt the remaining butter in a pan and cook the onion until soft. Add the mushrooms and cook for about 5 minutes more. Sprinkle with the Madeira and stir in the fromage frais and chives. Simmer for 1 to 2 minutes until heated through. Season to taste, spoon into the rolls, and serve hot.

MINI SEAFOOD BROCHETTES WITH MANGO MASH

Use conventional canned coconut milk or dilute the compressed blocks of creamed coconut sold in Asian grocery stores. To use the block variety, crumble 1 1/2 ounces into a heatproof measuring jug and pour in boiling water to make up to 5 ounces, stirring continuously until smooth. Do not use sweet coconut cream. Serves 4.

8 ounces monkfish fillet, skinned and cut into 8 chunks
8 raw jumbo shrimp, shelled, leaving tails intact
8 sea scallops

FOR THE MANGO MASH
2/3 cup coconut milk
1 garlic clove, crushed
1 small green chili, seeded and minced

1 mango, peeled, pitted, and chopped
Juice of 1 lime
2 tablespoons chopped fresh cilantro
Salt and freshly ground black pepper

To make the mango mash, place the coconut milk in a pan with the garlic and chili and simmer for 10 minutes. Leave to cool, then transfer to a food processor. Add the mango, lime juice, and cilantro and process until blended. Season and pour into a serving bowl.

Preheat the broiler. Thread the monkfish, shrimp, and scallops onto eight 6-inch bamboo skewers. Season and place on a lightly oiled broiler rack. Broil for 8 to 10 minutes, turning occasionally, until cooked and lightly browned. Serve at once, with the mango mash.

Mini Seafood Brochettes with Mango Mash

NIÇOISE PLATTER WITH GARLIC YOGURT

This is a variation of the classic French salad, and it looks striking with its combination of vibrant colors. Serve it with garlic toast, made by rubbing small slices of rustic-style bread with a halved garlic clove, drizzling them with olive oil and broiling until golden. Serves 4.

8 ounces green beans, trimmed	Juice of 1 small lemon
2 eggs	2/3 cup thick plain yogurt
4 ounces radishes	4-inch piece cucumber, seeded and diced
2 ripe plum tomatoes	1 garlic clove, crushed
1/2 cup pitted ripe olives	Salt and freshly ground black pepper

Add the green beans to a pan of boiling salted water and simmer for 3 minutes. Drain and refresh in cold running water. Bring another small pan of water to a boil. Add the eggs, return to a boil, and simmer gently for 7 minutes. Drain and cool under cold running water, then shell and cut in half.

Trim the radishes and cut in half if large. Cut the plum tomatoes into quarters. Arrange the beans, eggs, radishes, tomatoes, and olives on a serving platter. Sprinkle with the lemon juice and season to taste.

To make the garlic yogurt, mix together the yogurt, cucumber, and garlic in a small serving bowl and season well. Place on the platter and use as a dip for the vegetables.

MEDITERRANEAN VEGETABLE PLATTER WITH SALSA VERDE

To make sun-dried tomato paste, tip a jar of sun-dried tomatoes preserved in oil into a food processor and process until smooth. Return the paste to the jar, cover, and store in the refrigerator until required. Serves 4.

2 tablepoons olive oil	FOR THE SALSA VERDE
1 garlic clove, crushed	2 large plum tomatoes, peeled, seeded,
2 tablespoons sun-dried tomato paste	and diced
1 small eggplant, cut into 2-inch thick	1 green chili, seeded and minced
slices	2 tablespoons chopped fresh cilantro
1 small red and 1 small yellow bell pepper,	Juice of 1 lime
seeded and cut into quarters	
2 small zucchini, cut in half lengthwise	

Mix together the oil, garlic, and sun-dried tomato paste in a small bowl. Place the vegetables in a shallow nonmetallic dish and brush with the paste. Cover and leave to marinate for 30 minutes.

To make the salsa verde, mix together the tomatoes, chili, cilantro, and lime juice in a small serving bowl and set aside at room temperature.

Preheat the broiler. Arrange the vegetables on the broiler rack and broil for 10 to 15 minutes, turning them occasionally, until cooked through and slightly charred. Serve at once, with the salsa verde.

PICKLED HERRING AND MUSTARD TOASTS

Pickled herrings in jars are a good standby to have in the cupboard. As well as being delicious, they are low fat. Makes 24.

5 slices whole-wheat bread	2/3 cup thick plain yogurt
4 pickled herring fillets	Salt and freshly ground black pepper
2 tablespoons wholegrain mustard	24 tiny dill sprigs

Preheat the broiler. Using a 1 1/2-inch fluted cutter, stamp out 24 circles from the bread. Place on the broiler rack and lightly toast on both sides. Leave to cool on a wire rack.

Cut the herring into 24 1-inch pieces. Mix together the mustard, yogurt, and seasoning and spread over the toasts. Top each toast with a piece of herring and a dill sprig. Serve at once.

PROSCIUTTO AND MELON SKEWERS

This classic flavor combination looks good threaded onto small skewers or toothpicks. No cooking is required in this recipe. Makes 24.

12 thin slices prosciutto
1 large ripe melon, such as cantaloupe
24 small mint leaves

Cut each slice of prosciutto in half lengthwise. Cut the melon in half, scoop out the seeds, and peel away the skin. Cut the flesh into 72 equal pieces.

Fold each piece of prosciutto in half again lengthwise and thread it onto a skewer or toothpick, interweaving with 3 pieces of melon. Top with a mint leaf. Chill until required, but serve at room temperature.

GARLIC–AND–HERB STUFFED DATES

When buying dates, look for plump ones with smooth, shiny skins. The Medjool variety, grown in California, are considered by many connoisseurs to have the best flavor and texture. Makes 24.

24 large dates, about 1 pound	2 tablespoons chopped fresh herbs
1/2 cup low-fat cream cheese	Freshly ground black pepper
1/2 cup cottage cheese	1 tablespoon snipped fresh chives
1 garlic clove, crushed	

Split the dates along the top and remove the pits and any stem.

Mix together the low-fat cream cheese and cottage cheese. Beat in the garlic and herbs and season with lots of pepper. Fill each date with the garlic-and-herb mixture, using a small teaspoon.

Sprinkle the dates with the chives, arrange on a serving plate, and cover with plastic wrap. Chill for up to 2 hours before serving.

TERIYAKI SALMON WITH HORSERADISH DIP

Salmon scallopes—thin slices of boneless salmon—are the ideal cut for this Oriental-style recipe. Serves 4.

6 tablespoons light soy sauce
6 tablespoons sweet sherry
1 tablespoon soft brown sugar
1-inch piece fresh gingerroot, crushed
1 garlic clove, crushed

8 salmon scallopes, each 3 ounces, skinned
1 tablespoon white-wine vinegar
2 teaspoons creamed horseradish sauce
1 tablespoon sesame seeds

Put 4 tablespoons each of the soy sauce and sherry in a small pan with half the sugar, the ginger, and garlic and stir over low heat to dissolve the sugar. Bring to a boil, then simmer for about 5 minutes until reduced and thickened slightly. Leave to cool completely, then strain into a shallow nonmetallic dish.

Add the salmon to the soy marinade, stirring to coat. Cover and set aside for 30 minutes. Meanwhile, put the remaining soy sauce, sherry, and sugar in a small pan with the vinegar and cook over low heat until the sugar dissolves. Stir in the horseradish and keep warm.

Preheat the broiler. Thread each piece of salmon onto two 6-inch bamboo skewers and arrange on the lightly oiled broiler rack. Broil for 2 minutes, then turn over and brush with the remaining marinade. Sprinkle with the sesame seeds and broil for 2 to 3 minutes longer until the salmon is just cooked through. Serve at once, with the horseradish dip.

SWEET–AND–SOUR VEGETABLE KABOBS

It is easiest to brush the vegetables with the honey mixture while it is still warm. Any leftover honey mixture can be served with the kabobs as a dipping sauce. Serves 4.

5 tablespoons honey
4 tablespoons light soy sauce
4 tablespoons white wine vinegar
2 teaspoons grated fresh gingerroot
1 small fresh red chili, seeded and minced

1 red onion, cut into 1-inch pieces
2 red bell peppers, seeded and cut into 1-inch squares
8 yellow baby patty pan squash, halved
1 tablespoon sesame seeds

Place the honey, soy sauce, vinegar, ginger, and chili in a small pan with 1/2 cup water and bring to a boil. Reduce the heat and simmer for 5 to 10 minutes until thickened and well reduced.

Preheat the broiler. Thread the onion, peppers, and patty pan squash onto eight 6-inch bamboo skewers. Brush all over with the warm honey mixture and broil for about 15 minutes, turning frequently, until tender and lightly browned. Sprinkle with the sesame seeds and broil for 1 to 2 minutes longer until the seeds are lightly toasted. Serve at once.

CUCUMBER CUPS WITH TARAMASALATA

Taramasalata is a traditional Greek dip made from cod or other fish roe. Fresh roe, considered a delicacy by many and a popular ingredient all along the Mediterranean, is available in the spring. Makes 24.

6 slices whole-wheat bread
1 cucumber, peeled

FOR THE TARAMASALATA
4 ounces smoked cod roe
1 small garlic clove, crushed
1/2 cup fresh white bread crumbs
1 small shallot, chopped

Grated peel and juice of 1 small lemon
2 tablespoons olive oil
Freshly ground black pepper

To make the taramasalata, break up the cod roe, place it in a food processor, and process to a purée. Add the garlic, bread crumbs, shallot, and lemon peel and juice and blend again until smooth. Mix the oil with 3 tablespoons hot water and pour into the food processor, with the motor running. Season with pepper. Cover and chill until ready to use.

Preheat the broiler. Using a fluted cutter about the same diameter as the cucumber, cut out 24 circles of bread. Lightly broil them to toast on both sides. Leave to cool on a wire rack.

Cut the cucumber across into 24 slices and remove the seeds, using a teaspoon or an apple corer. Then cut down the sides of each slice with the fluted cutter. Spread each circle of toasted bread with a little of the taramasalata. Top with a piece of cucumber and spoon the taramasalata into the middle. Serve at once.

TAPENADE AND TOMATO CROSTINI

Add a little more lemon juice if it is necessary to bind the olive mixture; no oil is needed. Makes 24.

1 thin French baguette
1 garlic clove, halved
1 cup pitted ripe olives
2 anchovy fillets in oil, drained, rinsed, and chopped

1/3 can (6-ounce) tuna in water, drained
3 tablespoons chopped fresh parsley
2 tablespoons lemon juice
Salt and freshly ground black pepper
1 1/2 cups sliced small ripe tomatoes

Preheat the broiler. Cut the baguette into 24 slices, discarding the ends. Rub one side of each slice with the halved garlic clove (keep the garlic) and broil for 8 to 10 minutes, turning once, until golden. Leave to cool on a wire rack.

Place the garlic clove in a food processor with the olives, anchovies, tuna, 1 tablespoon of the parsley and 1 tablespoon of the lemon juice. Blend until fairly smooth, adding extra lemon juice if necessary. Season to taste.

Spread the toasts with the tapenade and arrange tomato slices on top. Season with pepper, sprinkle with the remaining parsley, and serve.

BREAD BITES

For many people, sandwiches are everyday fare, but that is no reason to be restricted to the dull deli variety that is so often the disappointing fall back. This chapter is full of sensational recipes for sandwiches, using a vaiety of different breads to encourage experimentation. These ingenius flavor combinations give new life to the old standard, and many of these sandwiches can easily be "miniaturized" to become party finger food. All recipes serve 4.

EGGPLANT AND PESTO MELTS IN FOCACCIA

This has to be one of the best-tasting vegetarian sandwiches ever! The eggplant, pesto, and cheese can be assembled up to 24 hours in advance, then covered and chilled until it is time to broil.

1 large eggplant	*5 ounces mozzarella cheese*
3 tablespoons olive oil	*2 tablespoons bottled pesto sauce*
Salt and freshly ground black pepper	*1 loaf Italian focaccia*
2 plum tomatoes	*1 garlic clove, halved*

Preheat the broiler. Cut the eggplant lengthwise into 4 long slices, discarding the ends. Brush each slice on both sides with a little of the oil, season generously, and broil for about 10 minutes, turning over occasionally, until soft and light golden.

Cut each tomato into 4 slices, discarding the ends. Cut the mozzarella cheese into 4 slices. Spread one side of each slice of eggplant with pesto, then arrange 2 slices of tomato and a slice of mozzarella on top. Bring the sides of the eggplant up around the filling and secure with a wooden toothpick.

Cut the focaccia into 4 pieces and split each one in half horizontally. Brush with the remaining oil and rub with the garlic clove. Broil the eggplant packages for 3 to 4 minutes, then add the focaccia and broil for 1 to 2 minutes longer until the bread is toasted and the mozzarella has begun to melt. Remove the toothpicks from the eggplant packages and sandwich each one between 2 pieces of focaccia. Serve hot.

CREAMED MUSHROOMS ON BRIOCHE TOASTS

Cultivated "wild" mushrooms are widely available in supermarkets, making a once very expensive ingredient affordable. This makes it possible to experiment with endless flavor combinations in this dish.

1 brioche	*1 tablespoon brandy*
3 tablespoons butter	*6 tablespoons crème fraîche*
5 cups sliced mixed wild mushrooms	*1 tablespoon chopped fresh tarragon*
Salt and freshly ground black pepper	*1 tablespoon chopped fresh flat-leaf parsley*

Cut the brioche into 4 thick slices, discarding the ends; set aside. Melt the butter in a skillet, add the mushrooms, and stir-fry for about 5 minutes. Season to taste.

Lightly toast the brioche slices and arrange on serving plates; keep warm. Add the brandy and crème fraîche to the mushrooms, stirring. Simmer for a few minutes until thicker, then stir in the tarragon. Spoon the mushroom mixture over the brioche toasts, scatter with the parsley, and serve at once.

PASTRAMI, DILL PICKLE, AND MUSTARD MAYO ON SOURDOUGH

Pastrami is the underside, or brisket, of beef, cured in a mixture of sugar, spices, and garlic for about seven days. It is then smoked, to produce the characteristic flavor, before being cooked.

1 small round sourdough loaf	*2 tablespoons mustard*
2 tablespoons butter, softened	*2 tablespoons mayonnaise*
12 thin slices pastrami	*Salt and freshly ground black pepper*
4 dill pickles	*Crinkle-cut potato chips, to serve*

Cut the sourdough loaf into 8 slices, discarding the ends, and spread with the butter. Arrange 3 slices of pastrami on each of 4 slices of bread, in an overlapping layer. Thinly slice the dill pickles and scatter over the pastrami.

Mix the mustard with the mayonnaise and season to taste. Thickly spread the remaining slices of bread with the mustard-flavored mayonnaise and use to cover the pastrami and dill pickles. Cut the sandwiches in half and serve with potato chips.

Roquefort, Grape, and Radicchio on Walnut Bread

BAGELS WITH SMOKED TROUT RILLETTES

Inexpensive smoked trout trimmings, sold at some supermarket fish counters and by fish merchants, are ideal to use in this recipe. To vary the flavor, use a mixture of fresh and smoked salmon. The rillettes can be frozen for up to one month, but should be completely thawed at room temperature before using.

6 ounces rainbow trout fillet	Juice of 1/2 lemon
6 tablespoons dry white wine	Good pinch of cayenne pepper
1 bay leaf	Salt and freshly ground black pepper
A few black peppercorns	4 bagels, split
3/4 cup unsalted butter, softened	1 tablespoon snipped fresh chives
6 ounces smoked trout	

Place the fresh trout in a pan with the wine, bay leaf, and peppercorns. Add enough water to cover and simmer for about 5 minutes until just tender and cooked through. Leave to cool in the liquid.

Melt 4 tablespoons of the butter in a skillet and cook the smoked trout until it turns pale pink; set aside to cool.

Drain the fresh trout, remove the skin, and flake the flesh. Break up the smoked trout and add to the fresh trout. Beat in the remaining butter, the lemon juice, cayenne pepper, and seasoning to taste.

Pile the trout rillettes on the bagel halves and sprinkle with the chives.

ROQUEFORT, GRAPE, AND RADICCHIO ON WALNUT BREAD

Roquefort cheese is creamy-white, semisoft, and crumbly with green/blue marbling. Do not buy any with a very white paste on the rind or too few veins. For the best flavor, let the cheese stand at room temperature for about one hour before using.

1 small walnut loaf	1 1/2 tablespoons olive oil
2 tablespoons butter, softened	1/2 tablespoon red-wine vinegar
10 ounces Roquefort cheese	Salt and freshly ground black pepper
1 small head radicchio, shredded	2 ounces seedless red grapes, halved

Cut the walnut loaf into 8 slices, discarding the ends, and lightly butter each slice. Cut off any rind from the Roquefort cheese and discard, then cut the cheese into thin slices. Arrange on 4 slices of bread.

Place the radicchio in a bowl and add the oil, vinegar, and seasoning. Toss to coat, then pile on top of the cheese. Scatter with the grapes and cover with the remaining slices of bread. Cut each sandwich in half on the diagonal before serving.

POACHED SALMON AND WATERCRESS MAYONNAISE ROLLS

To make this mayonnaise in a food processor or blender, it is necessary to double the quantity for most machines to work properly. Put the egg yolks, half the lemon juice, and the seasoning into the machine and blend for 10 seconds. Then, with the motor running at a low speed, pour in the oil in a thin stream. Stir in the remaining lemon juice with the grated peel and watercress.

2/3 cup dry white wine	Grated peel and juice of 1 lemon
A few parsley stems	Salt and freshly ground black pepper
1 bay leaf	6 tablespoons sunflower oil
A few black peppercorns	4 tablespoons finely chopped watercress
1 pound salmon fillet, skinned	2 tablespoons butter, softened
1 egg yolk	4 large whole-wheat rolls, split

Place the wine in a small pan with the parsley, bay leaf, and peppercorns. Add the salmon and pour in enough water to cover. Simmer very slowly for 5 minutes or until the fish is just cooked through and opaque; don't let the liquid boil or the fish will break up. Remove with a spatula and leave to cool. Break the poached salmon into large flakes.

Place the egg yolk in a bowl with half the lemon juice and seasoning. Whisk thoroughly. Add the oil, drop by drop to start, and then in a steady stream, whisking until the mayonnaise is thick and smooth. Stir in the watercress, lemon peel, and the remaining lemon juice.

Butter the rolls. Pile the salmon flakes on the bottom halves, spoon the watercress mayonnaise on top, and cover with the tops of the rolls. Serve at once.

CRISPY DUCK WITH MANGO RELISH ON MINI NAAN BREADS

Rubbing salt into the duck skin gives it a crisp texture. Naan breads— flat, yeasted Indian loaves that are traditionally baked on the side of *tandoor* ovens—are sold in Indian food stores. If the mini version is not available, quarter a regular-sized naan.

2 boneless duck breasts, each about	FOR THE MANGO RELISH
6 ounces	1 mango, peeled, pitted, and finely chopped
1 teaspoon salt	1 green chili, seeded and minced
1 tablespoon honey	1 shallot, minced
6 mini naan breads	Juice of 1 lime
1 cup shredded iceberg lettuce	1 teaspoon sugar

To make the mango relish, put the mango, chili, shallot, lime juice, and sugar in a small bowl and stir to combine. Cover with plastic wrap and chill until needed.

Preheat the oven to350°F. Prick the duck breasts all over with a fork and rub well with the salt. Place skin side up on a rack in a roasting pan. Roast for 15 minutes, then remove from the oven. Brush the skin with the honey, return to the oven, and roast for 20 minutes longer or until cooked through but still pink in the middle. Leave to rest for 5 minutes, then cut into thin slices.

Arrange the naan breads on a baking sheet and sprinkle with a little water. Warm in the oven for 2 to 3 minutes.

Split each naan in half and arrange 3 halves on each serving plate. Spread a little of the mango relish on each piece of naan and divide the lettuce between them. Arrange the duck slices on top in fan shapes and spoon a little more of the relish over each one. Serve with any remaining relish.

HOT KIPPER TOASTS

Also called kipper herring, kippers are dressed herring that have been cured and dry smoked. They have a golden brown skin and a rich smoky flavor. If unavailable, use another strong-flavored smoked fish, such as mackerel.

12 ounces kippers	1 teaspoon Worcestershire sauce
4 tablespoons fromage frais	1 loaf Italian ciabatta
3/4 cup grated Cheddar cheese	1 lemon, cut into wedges

Put the kippers into a large, heatproof pitcher and pour over enough boiling water to cover. Leave to stand for 5 minutes, then drain. Skin, remove any bones, and mash the flesh in a bowl. Stir in the fromage frais, Cheddar cheese, and Worcestershire sauce, stirring until blended.

Preheat the broiler. Cut the ciabatta into 12 slices on the diagonal, discarding the ends. Broil the ciabatta slices on both sides until lightly toasted. Top each slice with the kipper mixture and return to the broiler until bubbling. Squeeze over a little lemon juice and serve.

CURRIED TURKEY WITH APRICOT ON WHOLE-WHEAT BREAD

Korma curry paste, available from Indian and some Asian food stores, has a mild curry flavor. If you can't find any, cook 2 tablespoons mild curry powder with the onion for at least 5 minutes to eliminate the "raw" flavor of the spices. This recipe uses smoked turkey, but leftover roast turkey or chicken are also suitable.

4 tablespoons butter	2 tablespoons heavy cream
1 small onion, finely chopped	8 ounces smoked turkey
2 tablespoons korma curry paste	8 slices whole-wheat bread
2/3 cup dry white wine	1 cup shredded iceberg lettuce
1 tablespoon honey	4-inch piece cucumber, sliced
8 ready-to-eat dried apricots, finely chopped	4 scallions, minced
4 tablespoons mayonnaise	

Melt half the butter in a small pan and gently cook the onion until softened. Add the curry paste, wine, honey, and apricots and simmer, uncovered, for 15 to 20 minutes until almost all the liquid has evaporated. Leave to cool, then stir in the mayonnaise and cream. Remove any skin from the turkey and cut the meat into bite-sized pieces, then fold into the apricot mixture.

Lightly spread the bread with the remaining butter and divide the turkey mixture between 4 of the slices. Pile the iceberg lettuce on top and scatter with the cucumber and scallions. Top with the remaining bread. Cut each sandwich in half on the diagonal and serve.

WARM POLENTA AND WILD MUSHROOM SANDWICHES

The word polenta refers both to a form of porridge, popular throughout Italy, and the cornmeal used to make the dish. For this dish, use polenta from an Italian food store or yellow cornmeal.

1³/4 cups polenta or yellow cornmeal	2 shallots, sliced
Salt and freshly ground black pepper	5 cups sliced mixed wild mushrooms
6 tablespoons butter	2 teaspoons lemon juice
1 garlic clove, crushed	2 tablespoons chopped fresh parsley
1 tablespoon olive oil, plus extra for greasing	

Bring 1¹/2 quarts cold water to a boil in a large pan. Add 1 teaspoon salt and pour in the polenta in a continuous thin stream, stirring constantly with a wooden spoon. Simmer until the mixture is thick and no longer grainy, stirring frequently.

Remove the pan from the heat and stir in half the butter and the garlic. Season with pepper. Turn out into a lightly oiled baking tray or onto a wooden board and spread out into a 15 x 10-inch rectangle, about ¹/2 inch thick. Leave to cool, then cover and chill for at least 1 hour.

Preheat the broiler. Using a 3-inch round cutter, stamp out 8 circles from the set polenta. Brush them lightly with oil and place on the foil-lined broiler pan. Broil for 3 to 4 minutes on each side. Cover loosely and keep warm.

Melt the remaining butter in a large skillet and sauté the shallots for 2 minutes. Add the mushrooms and sauté for 3 to 4 minutes longer. Add the lemon juice and parsley and stir to mix together well.

Arrange 4 of the polenta circles on warmed serving plates and divide the mushroom mixture between them. Place the remaining polenta circles on top and serve.

PORK, BEET, AND HORSERADISH ON LIGHT RYE

These sandwiches are best when the pork is still warm. Don't try to make them in advance because the beet will run and color the meat and bread.

1¹/2 pounds loin of pork	2 tablespoons butter, softened
2 teaspoons chopped fresh rosemary needles	8 slices light rye bread
2 tablespoons Dijon mustard	2 tablespoons creamed horseradish
2 tablespoons lemon juice	2 cooked beets, thinly sliced
4 tablespoons honey	

Preheat the oven to 400°F. Remove the chine bone (backbone) from the loin of pork and cut off the rib bones, or ask the butcher at the meat counter to do this for you. Place the pork in a small roasting pan and roast for 30 minutes.

Meanwhile, mix together the rosemary needles, mustard, lemon juice, and honey.

Remove the pork from the oven and brush the rosemary and mustard glaze all over. Return the pork to the oven and continue roasting for 15 minutes longer, basting occasionally with the glaze, until browned, cooked through, and tender. Leave to rest for 15 minutes before slicing.

Lightly butter the bread and smear with the horseradish. Arrange the slices of pork on 4 of the bread slices and top with the beet slices. Cover with the remaining bread and cut in half to serve.

SUN-DRIED TOMATO, AVOCADO, AND MOZZARELLA ON FOCACCIA

Based on the classic Italian tomato, avocado, and mozzarella salad, this sandwich is good in the winter when fresh tomatoes have lost their intense flavor.

12 sun-dried tomatoes preserved in oil, drained with the oil reserved	1 loaf Italian focaccia
4 tablespoons bottled pesto sauce	10 ounces mozzarella cheese, thinly sliced
2 teaspoons lemon juice	1 large avocado, pitted and sliced
	Freshly ground black pepper

Cut the drained tomatoes into slivers. Place the reserved oil from the tomatoes in a bowl and stir in the pesto sauce and lemon juice until thoroughly mixed. Cut the focaccia in half horizontally and spread the pesto mixture on the cut surfaces.

Arrange the mozzarella on one piece of focaccia and scatter with the tomato slivers. Put the avocado slices on top and season with plenty of pepper. Sandwich the focaccia together and press down lightly. Cut into 4 equal pieces and serve.

Sun-Dried Tomato, Avocado, and Mozzarella on Focaccia

THE CLASSIC CLUB SANDWICH

The popularity of this double-decker has stood the test of time, never falling from favor since it was first enjoyed around the beginning of this century. Vary the ingredients, depending on what is available.

1 tablespoon wholegrain mustard
6 tablespoons mayonnaise
Salt and freshly ground black pepper
8 slices smoked bacon
8 slices white bread
4 slices whole-wheat bread

1/2 cup finely shredded iceberg lettuce
2 tomatoes, sliced
1 small white salad onion, cut into
wafer-thin slices
4 ounces wafer-thin sliced chicken
4 thin slices Gruyère cheese

Mix the mustard, mayonnaise, and seasoning in a small bowl. Preheat the broiler. Broil the bacon until crisp; crumble coarsely or chop it. Lightly toast all the bread, then spread with the mustard mayonnaise.

Divide half the lettuce between 4 slices of white bread, top with the tomato and half the onion slices, and season to taste. Cover with the chicken and add the whole-wheat bread slices, mayonnaise side up.

Pile the remaining lettuce on top and add the cheese slices. Scatter with the bacon and the remaining onion. Cover with the remaining white bread slices, mayonnaise side down, and press down lightly. Cut each sandwich into 4 triangles and secure each piece with a toothpick or small plastic skewer. Serve at once.

ROAST BEEF AND ARUGULA ON RYE WITH MUSTARD DRESSING

Use the tip of a small sharp knife to make the incisions in the beef for the garlic slivers. The rich flavor of rye bread, sometimes called black bread, is the perfect accompaniment for beef.

12 ounces beef tenderloin
1 large garlic clove, cut into slivers
Salt and freshly ground black pepper
4 tablespoons sunflower oil
1 tablespoon walnut oil

1 tablespoon white-wine vinegar
2 teaspoons Dijon mustard
3 ounces tender young arugula leaves
2 tablespoons butter, softened
8 slices rye bread

Preheat the oven to 450°F. Remove the beef from the refrigerator and leave it to reach room temperature. Stud it with the garlic slivers and season all over. Heat 2 tablespoons of the sunflower oil in a skillet until very hot and cook the beef for 1 minute on each side to seal.

Transfer the beef to a small roasting pan and roast for 20 minutes. Remove from the oven and leave to rest for 10 minutes before cutting into thin slices, discarding the slivers of garlic.

To make the dressing, place the remaining sunflower oil, the walnut oil, vinegar, mustard, and seasoning in a screw-top jar and shake well. Place the arugula in a bowl, add the dressing, and toss to coat.

Lightly butter the rye bread and divide the beef slices between 4 of them. Pile on the dressed arugula and top with the remaining bread. Cut each sandwich in half on the diagonal and serve.

MUFFULETTA

Originally from New Orleans, this hero-style sandwich is perfect for picnics because it's easy to transport, or to serve as part of a buffet for an informal get-together. Serves 8 to 10.

2 small eggplants, sliced lengthwise
4 small zucchini, sliced lengthwise
Olive oil, for brushing
2 yellow bell peppers, seeded and
quartered
1 round loaf, such as Italian pugliese
1 garlic clove, halved
6 tablespoons bottled pesto sauce

3/4 cup drained sun-dried tomatoes
preserved in oil
14 ounces mozzarella cheese,
thinly sliced
8 ounces garlic salami, thinly sliced with
rind removed
6 ounces tender young spinach leaves
Salt and freshly ground black pepper

Preheat the broiler. Brush the eggplant and zucchini slices with oil and arrange on the broiler rack with the peppers. Broil for 8 to 10 minutes, turning over the eggplant and zucchini slices occasionally, until tender and lightly browned. When the pepper skins are charred, wrap the peppers in plastic wrap and leave to cool, with the other vegetables. When cool, peel off and discard the pepper skins.

Cut the top off the loaf of bread, then hollow out the middle, leaving a shell 1 inch thick. Rub the inside of the bread all over with the garlic and then spread with the pesto sauce.

Arrange the eggplant slices in an overlapping layer on the bottom of the bread shell and scatter with the sun-dried tomatoes. Add the zucchini, followed by the mozzarella cheese, salami, and the peppers, seasoning each layer generously. Add the spinach, and replace the top of the loaf. Wrap tightly in plastic wrap and chill overnight, pressed down by a heavy weight. Unwrap, cut into thick wedges, and serve.

CROQUE MONSIEUR CROISSANTS

To use the chilled croissant dough, instead of baked croissants, follow the directions for baking on the package, placing the filling in the center of each croissant and adding 15 minutes to the recommended baking time.

4 fresh croissants
1 tablespoon Dijon mustard
4 thin slices roast ham, cut into strips

1 1/4 cups grated Gruyère cheese
Freshly ground black pepper
2 tablespoons butter, diced

Preheat the broiler. Split each croissant in half horizontally, not cutting all the way through. Spread the mustard thinly over the open croissants and scatter with the ham. Add 1/4 cup cheese to each croissant and season with pepper.

Broil the open croissants for 2 to 3 minutes until the cheese is bubbling and melted. Close up each croissant and sprinkle with the remaining cheese. Dot with the butter and broil for 1 to 2 minutes longer. Serve at once.

EGG AND BACON MUFFINS WITH PAN-FRIED TOMATOES

These are the perfect late-night snack or early morning "pick-me-up." If you don't have any metal round cookie or biscuit cutters, which give the eggs a perfect round shape, just let the fried eggs drape over the top of the muffins.

2 large ripe tomatoes	*4 eggs*
2 teaspoons seasoned flour	*2 English muffins, split*
4 tablespoons sunflower oil	*2 tablespoons butter, softened*
8 slices smoked slab bacon	*Salt and freshly ground black pepper*

Preheat the oven to its lowest setting. Cut each tomato into 6 slices, discarding the ends. Place the seasoned flour on a plate and dip in the tomato slices to coat lightly. Heat half the oil in a large skillet and cook the tomato slices for about 1 minute on each side. Remove from the pan and keep warm.

Preheat the broiler. Broil the bacon until cooked through and crisp. Keep warm.

Place four 3-inch metal round cutters in the skillet with the remaining oil and heat until very hot. Break an egg into each cutter and cook for 2 to 3 minutes, spooning the oil over the yolks until they are just set.

Meanwhile, lightly toast the muffins and spread with the butter. Place 2 bacon slices on each muffin half and arrange 3 slices of pan-fried tomato in an overlapping layer on top. Remove the skillet from the heat and carefully lift out the metal cutters. Top each muffin with an egg, season to taste, and serve at once.

MARINATED STEAK BAGUETTES

The broiling time in this recipe produces a medium-rare steak, but broil for 2 minutes on each side for a rare steak and 6 to 7 minutes on each side for well-done steak.

4 sirloin steaks, each about 4 ounces	*1 large garlic clove, crushed*
and 3/4 inch thick	*1 teaspoon fresh thyme leaves*
Salt and freshly ground black pepper	*4 x 4-inch pieces French baguette, split*
3 tablespoons olive oil	*2 tablespoons Dijon mustard*
1 tablespoon red-wine vinegar	*Frisée lettuce, torn into small pieces*

Trim any fat off the steaks, season well, and place in a nonmetallic dish. Mix together the olive oil, red-wine vinegar, garlic, and thyme and spoon over the steaks, turning each piece to coat. Cover and marinate in the refrigerator for at least 30 minutes or up to 24 hours.

Preheat the broiler. Shake the steaks to remove any excess marinade and broil for 3 to 4 minutes on each side. Meanwhile, lightly toast the baguette slices.

Spread each slice of baguette with the mustard, then sandwich a steak and some lettuce between 2 halves. Serve at once.

PEPERONATA WITH GOAT CHEESE ON CIABATTA

Inspired by peperonata, the popular Mediterranean sautéed pepper dish, this sandwich pairs the sweetness of bell peppers with the creaminess of goat cheese to make an outstanding flavor combination.

4 tablespoons chili oil	*1 large garlic clove, crushed*
1 red and 1 yellow bell pepper, seeded and	*3 ounces round goat cheese*
thinly sliced	*1 loaf Italian ciabatta bread*
2 teaspoons cumin seeds	*1 tablespoon chopped fresh parsley*
Salt and freshly ground black pepper	

Heat the oil in a large, heavy-based skillet, add the peppers and cumin seeds, and sauté over high heat for 2 to 3 minutes. Season generously, then reduce the heat and stir in the garlic. Cook for 10 minutes longer, stirring occasionally, until the peppers have caramelized around the edges. Leave to cool slightly.

Cut the goat cheese into 4 slices. Cut the ciabatta in half horizontally and then across to make 4 pieces. Spread the pepper mixture on the cut surfaces of the bread and place a slice of goat cheese on top. Sprinkle with parsley and serve.

SAUSAGE HEROS WITH CARAMELIZED ONIONS

This is a real kid's favorite, and is great served with french fries. The sausages can also be grilled on the barbecue for the same length of time.

4 good-quality thick pork link sausages	*FOR THE BARBECUE SAUCE*
1 onion, cut into thick slices	*6 tablespoons tomato ketchup*
1 tablespoon seasoned flour	*1 tablespoon each soy sauce and lemon juice*
2 tablespoons sunflower oil	*1 teaspoon each Dijon mustard and honey*
4 long crusty white rolls	
1/2 cup shredded iceberg lettuce	

To make the barbecue sauce, mix all the ingredients in a small bowl.

Preheat the broiler. Place the sausages in a small nonmetallic baking dish. Add half the barbecue sauce and spread it evenly all over the sausages. Broil the sausages for 10 to 15 minutes, turning them over and basting occasionally with any sauce left in the dish.

Meanwhile, separate the onion into rings and dust with the seasoned flour. Heat the oil in a skillet and cook the onion rings until crisp and golden. Remove with a slotted spoon and drain on paper towels.

Split the rolls lengthwise and fill them with the lettuce. Lay the sausages on top, and drizzle with the remaining barbecue sauce. Scatter the onion rings over the top and serve hot.

RECIPE INDEX

Asparagus borek 30

Asparagus with crab and lemon dip 44

Bagels with smoked trout rillettes 54

Bagna cauda 38

Blood sausage with apple 28

Broiled squid with feta 42

Caviar canapés 26

Cheese and olive sablé shapes 32

Chicken liver pâté toasts with onion conserve 32

Chinese egg rolls 17

Chinese spiced spareribs 18

Corn and chili cornbread muffins 20

Corn fritters with sweet chili sauce 34

Creamed mushrooms on brioche toasts 52

Crispy duck with mango relish on mini naan breads 55

Crispy mushrooms with goat cheese dip 37

Crispy new potatoes with mustard relish 38

Croque monsieur croissants 58

Cucumber cups with taramasalata 50

Curried turkey with apricot on whole-wheat bread 55

Deviled chicken wings 20

Egg and bacon muffins with pan-fried tomatoes 60

Eggplant and pesto melts in focaccia 52

Empanadas 20

Falafel with yogurt-mint relish 44

French-style stuffed mussels 32

Fried eggplant with skordalia 37

Fried cauliflower florets with romesco sauce 20

Fritto misto 34

Garlic-and-herb stuffed dates 48

Garlic and lemon mushrooms 42

Garlic pita fingers with taramasalata 34

Grape leaf bundles with goat cheese and olives 30

Guacamole with roasted peppers and chili tortilla chips 17

Honey-glazed chicken tikka mini kabobs 46

Hot-and-sour noodle-wrapped shrimp 18

Hot kipper toasts 55

Jumbo shrimp with tricolor dip 46

Marinated Greek olives 46

Marinated halloumi cheese and tomato kabobs 26

Marinated steak baguettes 60

Mediterranean vegetable platter with salsa verde 48

Melted cheese and corn nachos 36

Mexican lamb fajitas 16

Mini boeuf en croute 24

Mini potato patties with bacon and blue cheese 28

Mini samosas with mint and cilantro chutney 22

Mini seafood brochettes with mango mash 47

Mini spanakopitta purses 27

Miniature salmon balls with lemon-butter sauce 30

Miniature savory choux puffs 28

Mixed mushroom baskets 47

Mixed satay skewers 22

Mozzarella fritters with spicy tomato sauce 38

Muffuletta 58

Niçoise platter with garlic yogurt 48

Pancetta and Gruyère tartlets 26

Pastrami, dill pickle, and mustard mayo on sourdough 52

Peperonata with goat cheese on ciabatta 60

Persian broiled baby eggplant 44

Pesto pastry twists 27

Pickled herring and mustard toasts 48

Plantain fries with tamarind chutney 22

Poached salmon and watercress mayonnaise rolls 54

Polenta crackers with roasted tomato salsa 14

Pork, beet, and horseradish on light rye 56

Potato skins with avocado and red onion salsa 47

Potato wedges with fresh cilantro chutney 18

Prosciutto and arugula crostini 30

Prosciutto and melon skewers 48

Quick mozzarella and salami pizzas 37

Roast beef and arugula on rye with mustard dressing 58

Roquefort, grape, and radicchio on walnut bread 54

Salt cod fritters with sweet pepper sauce 24

Sausage and herb nuggets with apricot relish 36

Sausage heros with caramelized onions 60

Scones with smoked salmon and chives 28

Sizzling chorizo and cherry tomato kabobs 40

Spanish omelet wedges 40

Spiced lamb kabobs with tzatziki 18

Steamed baby vegetables with hollandaise sauce 42

Sun-dried tomato and chicken bites with basil mayonnaise 27

Sun-dried tomato, avocado, and mozzarella on focaccia 56

Sweet-and-sour vegetable kabobs 50

Sweet potato slices with chili-butter dip 16

Sweet potato sticks with blue cheese dip 36

Swiss cheese fondue 40

Tabbouleh party pita pockets 47

Tapenade and tomato crostini 50

Teriyaki salmon with horseradish dip 50

Thai crab bites with spiced coconut dip 14

The classic club sandwich 58

Toasted polenta fingers with dolcelatte sauce 32

Turkey and cherry tomato twists 44

Turkey wontons 22

Vegetable bhajias with tomato chutney 17

Vegetable chips with sour cream dip 40

Vegetable tempura with chili dipping sauce 16

Warm polenta and wild mushroom sandwiches 56

Zucchini fritters with red pesto sauce 42

First published in the United States of America in 1996 by
Rizzoli International Publications, Inc.
300 Park Avenue South, New York, NY 10010

First published in Great Britain in 1996 by
George Weidenfeld & Nicolson Limited
The Orion Publishing Group

ISBN 0-8478-1938-8
LC 95-72944

Designed by The Design Revolution, Brighton
Printed and bound in Italy